A Disequilibrium Model of Demand
for Factors of Production

NATIONAL BUREAU OF ECONOMIC RESEARCH

NUMBER 99

GENERAL SERIES

A Disequilibrium Model of Demand for Factors of Production

M. ISHAQ NADIRI

National Bureau of Economic Research and
New York University

AND

SHERWIN ROSEN

National Bureau of Economic Research and
University of Rochester

National Bureau of Economic Research
NEW YORK
1973

Distributed by Columbia University Press
NEW YORK AND LONDON

RELATION OF THE DIRECTORS
TO THE WORK AND PUBLICATIONS
OF THE NATIONAL BUREAU OF ECONOMIC RESEARCH

1. The object of the National Bureau of Economic Research is to ascertain and to present to the public important economic facts and their interpretation in a scientific and impartial manner. The Board of Directors is charged with the responsibility of ensuring that the work of the National Bureau is carried on in strict conformity with this object.

2. The President of the National Bureau shall submit to the Board of Directors, or to its Executive Committee, for their formal adoption all specific proposals for research to be instituted.

3. No research report shall be published until the President shall have submitted to each member of the Board the manuscript proposed for publication, and such information as will, in his opinion and in the opinion of the author, serve to determine the suitability of the report for publication in accordance with the principles of the National Bureau. Each manuscript shall contain a summary drawing attention to the nature and treatment of the problem studied, the character of the data and their utilization in the report, and the main conclusions reached.

4. For each manuscript so submitted, a special committee of the Directors (including Directors Emeriti) shall be appointed by majority agreement of the President and Vice Presidents (or by the Executive Committee in case of inability to decide on the part of the President and Vice Presidents), consisting of three Directors selected as nearly as may be one from each general division of the Board. The names of the special manuscript committee shall be stated to each Director when the manuscript is submitted to him. It shall be the duty of each member of the special manuscript committee to read the manuscript. If each member of the manuscript committee signifies his approval within thirty days of the transmittal of the manuscript, the report may be published. If at the end of that period any member of the manuscript committee withholds his approval, the President shall then notify each member of the Board, requesting approval or disapproval of publication, and thirty days additional shall be granted for this purpose. The manuscript shall then not be published unless at least a majority of the entire Board who shall have voted on the proposal within the time fixed for the receipt of votes shall have approved.

5. No manuscript may be published, though approved by each member of the special manuscript committee, until forty-five days have elapsed from the transmittal of the report in manuscript form. The interval is allowed for the receipt of any memorandum of dissent or reservation, together with a brief statement of his reasons, that any member may wish to express; and such memorandum of dissent or reservation shall be published with the manuscript if he so desires. Publication does not, however, imply that each member of the Board has read the manuscript, or that either members of the Board in general or the special committee have passed on its validity in every detail.

6. Publications of the National Bureau issued for informational purposes concerning the work of the Bureau and its staff, or issued to inform the public of activities of Bureau staff, and volumes issued as a result of various conferences involving the National Bureau shall contain a specific disclaimer noting that such publication has not passed through the normal review procedures required in this resolution. The Executive Committee of the Board is charged with review of all such publications from time to time to ensure that they do not take on the character of formal research reports of the National Bureau, requiring formal Board approval.

7. Unless otherwise determined by the Board or exempted by the terms of paragraph 6, a copy of this resolution shall be printed in each National Bureau publication.

(Resolution adopted October 25, 1926 and revised February 6, 1933,
February 24, 1941, April 20, 1968, and September 17, 1973)

Contents

Tables

Tables

Charts

Figures

PREFACE

THE behavior of capital investment and employment patterns in time-series data has been an active area of research in economics for many years, undoubtedly because of the importance of these phenomena for understanding and controlling business cycles. Research in the area has intensified in the past decade, with the emergence of better data and the realization that investment and employment variations may be best understood in terms of a modification of the theory of the firm. The modification largely consists of explicit recognition that there are costs associated with changes in the stocks of inputs as well as with changes in the intensity of their use. Under these circumstances, rational decision-making requires taking into account the effect of current decisions on future events, for there are strong incentives to minimize costs of change through production smoothing, reducing the period-to-period variance of input stocks by spreading out such changes over an extended horizon. By providing a link between present and future, this approach introduces a dynamic element into the theory of the firm that the static constructs of short- and long-run cost functions lack. It focuses attention away from the question of which inputs are to be regarded as fixed or variable over the period spanned by the data, and toward the role of inventories of both output and inputs and of utilization rates, and the dynamic linkages between input changes during the adjustment process. We hope to have provided new evidence on these important and interesting relationships in this study.

A great deal of research under the auspices of the National Bureau has pointed toward the development of dynamic models of the variety illustrated in this monograph. In particular, mention must be made of

Wesley Mitchell's[1] view of the behavior of costs in the generation of business cycles and empirical work by Thor Hultgren[2] in documenting that behavior for the case of labor costs. Further work by Hultgren[3] and also by Solomon Fabricant[4] traced systematic patterns of productivity over the course of business cycles and raised questions difficult to resolve on the basis of the customary distinctions between the short run and the long run. Finally, Gerhard Bry's[5] investigation of variations in the length of the work week naturally lead toward input inventory and capacity considerations in the theory of demand for factors of production. Though sometimes only implicitly, elements of all these works are to be found in our model, and our research certainly could not have proceeded as it did without them.

Our collaboration began in 1967–68, when we both held research fellowships at the National Bureau and decided ,to pool our efforts. From the beginning, many persons contributed to the completion of this volume, and we are greatly indebted to all of them. Geoffrey Moore, then director of research, and Victor Fuchs, then in charge of the fellowship program, gave much encouragement to our initial plans. At a later stage John Meyer made a number of important suggestions regarding model design. George Borts, Solomon Fabricant, Robert Lucas, Marc Nerlove, Arthur Treadway, and Neil Wallace offered many useful suggestions and criticism of the work at various times. A staff reading committee consisting of Robert Eisner, Franklin Fisher, and Christopher Sims provided a volume of constructive criticism that materially improved the manuscript. Robert Lipsey was also very helpful in this connection. We are also thankful for the valuable comments of the Board of Directors' reading committee: Otto Eckstein, Nathaniel Goldfinger, and Robert M. Solow. Our thanks also are due to Emilio G. Collado for his observations on the manuscript.

This study benefited greatly from highly competent assistance. Most of

---

1. Wesley C. Mitchell, *Business Cycles: The Problem and Its Setting*, New York, NBER, 1927.

2. Thor Hultgren, *Changes in Labor Cost During Cycles in Production and Business*, Occasional Paper 74, New York, NBER, 1960.

3. Thor Hultgren, *Cost, Prices, and Profits: Their Cyclical Relations*, New York, NBER, 1965.

4. Solomon Fabricant, *Basic Facts on Productivity Change*, Occasional Paper 63, New York, NBER, 1959.

5. Gerhard Bry, *The Average Workweek as an Economic Indicator*, Occasional Paper 69, New York, NBER, 1959.

the data processing and computations were supervised admirably by Veena Bhatia, Morris Harf, and Susan Johnson. They were assisted at one time or another by Margaret Crump, Jennifer Michaels, and Selma Seligsohn. Rose Ferro provided very efficient and conscientious typing and secretarial assistance. We are very grateful to Ester Moskowitz for editing the manuscript. H. Irving Forman's expert draftsmanship contributed immeasurably to the presentation of the material in this book.

Financing for the study was provided partly from grants to the National Bureau by the Alfred P. Sloan Foundation and the Alex C. Walker Educational and Charitable Foundation for the Bureau's studies on productivity, employment, and price levels, and partly from the general funds of the National Bureau.

INTRODUCTION

THE purpose of this volume is to present a systematic investigation of investment, employment, utilization rates, and inventories in manufacturing industries over the post-World War II period. The focus of the study is on the dynamic interrelationships among these variables that arise from changing demand and market conditions. Costs associated with changes of these variables, absent in a static world, significantly affect the outcome in a dynamic setting. These costs provide a link between present and future profits and consequently require firms to take explicit account of the effects of current decisions on future profits.

In a changing world, the firm is faced with three basic options regarding production and input. It can perfectly synchronize input and output decisions without holding any inventories. It can hold inventories of output to meet changing demand and stabilize employment of its capital stock and labor force. Finally, it can hold the equivalent of inventories of inputs, not smoothing production perfectly but changing the intensity of use of existing resources. The first strategy is unlikely to be pursued because there are natural delays in production and because rapid acquisition and change in the utilization of inputs is costly. The typical policy for most firms is to follow a mixed strategy of holding some inventories of output and some of input. The combination is determined by an interrelated set of implicit cost trade-offs which are, in turn, determined by the technological and market conditions under which the firm operates.

The forces underlying these trade-offs are very complex, and lead to a network of interrelated decisions. Changing the levels of output inventories, input utilization rates, or additions to input stocks all involve costs which vary according to the type of adjustments, the length of time, and the decisions made about the other inputs and outputs. These events, in turn, lead to a pattern of intertemporal substitutions among these variables. Costs of altering input utilization rates include overtime wage payments to labor and accelerated depreciation of capital equipment because it is used more intensively. Finally, changing the labor force involves search, hiring, and training costs, and acquiring new capital goods entails order delays, installation costs, etc.

Some simple examples will illustrate the nature of the response mechanisms involved. Suppose a firm expects a permanent increase in sales, which will eventually make an expansion of its productive capacity advantageous. To meet new demand in the short run requires, because of adjustment delays in the acquisition of new capital goods, increasing utilization of existing capacity by adding overtime and additional labor and by running down existing inventories. Current costs are thereby increased temporarily. As capital expansion proceeds, these costs are slowly reduced to more normal levels. In certain cases, the firm may be additionally constrained by labor market conditions. Current unavailability of skilled labor at or near existing wage rates leads to the postponement of capital expansion plans and greater reliance on more intensive utilization of existing resources. In situations where increased sales are not considered permanent, costs of temporary changes of plant capacity may be so large that new investments are precluded. The firm increases utilization of existing stocks and may temporarily increase its labor force as well. As sales fall to their prior levels, utilization rates taper off, inventory-sales ratios slowly increase to their desired levels, and temporary labor acquisitions are reduced.

It is important to take account of these interrelationships and feedbacks in the adjustment process, both from a purely scientific point of view and also for policy prescriptions. The scientific contribution lies in a more complete description and analysis of production decisions. Taking account of these dynamic constraints provides an opportunity to predict more accurately the production and factor employment behavior of firms. This point is illustrated by a survey of the literature on investment and employment functions. Existing time-series employment studies assume fixed capital stock. Yet estimated labor stock adjustment periods are so long as to place this assumption in serious doubt. On the other hand, most investment studies treat labor as a completely variable factor even though employment studies indicate otherwise. Furthermore, few of these investigations have made adequate allowance for variations in utilization rates of labor and capital, and the estimates often are difficult to interpret.[1]

The relationships among input and output decisions have important policy implications. For example, a policy designed primarily to influence investment behavior may have unintended spillover effects on employment and utilization decisions. Policies aimed at one market do not in fact remain confined to that market. An important consequence is that program monitoring of fiscal and monetary policies is rendered more difficult. Because of the complexity of the response networks involved, the immediate response and the evolution of the system can be very different from that intended. It therefore becomes very important to be able to predict how these response patterns will evolve. For example, as will be seen below, employment response to expansionary fiscal policy may exceed its ultimate equilibrium value for some period of time after the stimulus because of the feedback and cross-adjustment mechanisms involved. In terms of employment objectives, the policy temporarily may look better (or worse) than it will ultimately be.

An attempt has been made in this study to develop and estimate a model which takes explicit account of these interrelationships. The theoretical structure is based on the neoclassical theory of production in the presence of costs of changing input levels. The model and estimates of it provide a unified framework for analyzing input demand functions over time. The inputs considered are production and nonproduction labor, capital stock, and inventories. The role of utilization rates in these functions and variations in utilization rates are also analyzed. The model is estimated for total manufacturing and its component sub-sectors—durables, nondurables, and fifteen individual industries—using quarterly data over the 1947–69 period.

The main contribution of this study lies in four areas:

1. We have tested for the existence of cross-adjustment or feedback effects among input decisions and have found them to be present in all industries studied. Quarterly changes in each input are found to be

1. Some studies use man-hours rather than employment stock but do not determine the division between employment and hours of work. Two exceptions are Black and Kalejian [1970] and Kuh [1965a]. Nadiri [1969] explicitly takes into account capital utilization in his investment function, but it is exogenous to the model.

significantly affected by the position and adjustment response of other inputs. The results verify the generality of the model, which includes existing employment and investment models as special cases.

2. The existence of cross-input adjustment effects implies patterns of responses to changing conditions which are in marked contrast to results reported in previous studies. Two outstanding general features of the results are as follows: First, dynamic responses of utilization rate variables and, very often, employment variables overshoot their ultimate equilibrium values very soon after the adjustment process begins. These results cannot be obtained (by construction) in traditional employment and investment function studies, which exclude feedback effects from one input to the other. Second, there are systematic differences in the timing and speed of response among inputs. Utilization rates respond very quickly to changes in demand, followed by production employment and inventory variables. Nonproduction worker employment and especially capital stock respond very sluggishly. Moreover, the average lags in the system tend to be shorter than those found by previous investigators, who have ignored interaction effects. It should be emphasized that those variables which overshoot their ultimate equilibria are also the quickest to respond to external stimuli. They act as buffers, taking up the slack imposed by the slower-adjusting inputs such as capital. This result justifies the cross-adjustment specification of the model.

3. The analysis permits separation of sales and relative input price responses, and these are systematically different in all industries studied. The sales effects are much larger than the price effects, which tend to be very small in magnitude and often indiscernible in these data.

4. There are systematic differences across industries, both in speed of response of inputs to sales and prices and in the ultimate effects of these variables. Input responses are much more rapid in durable goods industries than in nondurables, and long-run responses are also smaller.

The material in this volume is presented as follows: Chapter 1 contains a discussion of the general setting of the problem and illustrations of some conceptual issues. The complete model is presented and elaborated in Chapter 2. The nature of the data and some preliminary observations are discussed in Chapter 3. Structural estimates, distributed lags, and long-run elasticities for total manufacturing and their interpretation are presented in Chapter 4. Results of various experiments with alternative forms of the model for total manufacturing are found in Chapter 5. The complete results for individual industries are presented in Chapter 6. In Chapter 7, the empirical results obtained in this study are used to answer some heretofore unresolved questions about the estimation of short-run employment and investment functions, and a summary and conclusions are also given. Appendixes and references are included at the end of the volume.

For those readers interested only in the essential theoretical and empirical results of this volume, we recommend Chapter 2 for theoretical development and Chapters 4, 6, and 7 for empirical application.

A Disequilibrium Model of Demand
for Factors of Production

1

NATURE OF THE PROBLEM AND RELATION TO THE LITERATURE

A. GENERAL CONSIDERATIONS

The theory of the firm shows how the demand for factors of production can be derived from knowledge of production functions and product and factor market conditions. Empirical investigations have pursued two broad lines of development. First is a series of cross-sectional studies involving direct estimation of production and cost functions on the one hand, and estimation of factor demand functions on the other (Nerlove [1967], Nadiri [1970]). Second is a vast literature using time-series data. Here attention has been divided between studies of long-term productivity (e.g., Denison [1962]) and employment of factors of production (e.g., Kuh [1965], Jorgenson [1963]). At least up until recent years, these strands have been pursued more or less independently.

The main conceptual differences between cross-sectional and time-series analyses rests on the assumption that cross-sectional observations largely reflect long-run optimizing behavior, whereas time-series observations do not. Although estimation of long-run profit-maximizing conditions may be appropriate to cross-sectional studies, no such case can be made for time series. Given the presence of large and uncertain variations in final demand and of short-run imperfections in factor and product markets, there is no reason to expect decision makers to maintain "long-run" desired input positions at every point in time. Instead, gradual adjustment to these positions is to be expected. For this reason, many economists use a partial adjustment or flexible accelerator model,

$$y_t - y_{t-1} = \beta(y_t^* - y_{t-1}), \tag{1.1}$$

where y_t represents the level of an input at time t, y_t^* is the long-run desired level of the input and β is an adjustment coefficient bounded by 0.0 and 1.0. Functions such as (1.1) have been estimated on a wide variety of time-series data for both capital or investment demand (Eisner [1960], Koyck [1954], Hickman [1965]) and demand for labor (Brechling [1965], Ball-St. Cyr [1966], Dhrymes [1969], Ireland-Smyth [1967], Nadiri [1969]). In most of these studies, the economic meaning of the adjustment mechanisms of (1.1) is not explicitly stated, but rests on an intuitive discussion of time delays, delivery lags, installation costs, and so on. By and large, these studies do not explicitly integrate the costs of changing input levels into functions for estimating factor demand; they also treat adjustments of each input separately and independently of adjustments of other inputs.

To set out the major issues and to indicate the potential contribution of the present work, a brief discussion of econometric time-series studies of employment and investment is provided below. Only the main issues are stated; interested readers can explore the details in original sources. A brief discussion of the time-series employment function is presented first, followed by a similar discussion of empirical investment functions. Finally, the framework of this study is illustrated with a simple example of a more general disequilibrium model of factor demand. That model is fully specified in Chapter 2 and estimated in subsequent chapters of this volume.

B. TIME-SERIES EMPLOYMENT MODELS

A great deal of research in the past ten years or so has been devoted to examination of time series of production and employment, especially the behavior of these variables over the course of business cycles. The data reveal that short-term fluctuations in real output tend to be greater in amplitude than corresponding fluctuations in employment. This difference in amplitude gives rise to systematic cyclical fluctuations in measured man-hour productivity. As output falls from its peak, man-hours employed falls less rapidly, causing declines in man-hours productivity near business cycle peaks; during recovery periods, on the other hand, output grows more rapidly than man-hours, with the result that average labor productivity increases. These phenomena, along with apparently sticky money wages, which display little systematic cyclical variability, "account" for corresponding cyclical fluctuations in factor shares over the course of business cycles. Labor's share of total product tends to grow during business cycle contractions and to fall during recovery periods. Part of this is due to systematic changes in labor quality over the cycle, but observation of this behavior has also given rise to various notions of "labor hoarding." It is maintained that firms tend to smooth employment variations over the course of the cycle, to economize on transactions costs involved in the recruitment of labor and in specific investments in their employees; that is, there are costs of adjustment or costs associated with changing employment that make it economical to stabilize employment fluctuations to some extent.

As an empirical matter, most studies of short-term employment behavior use a type of flexible accelerator or stock adjustment model that was widely used in earlier studies of investment behavior. In light of the excellent survey of most of this work by Fair [1969], detailed examination of the differences among all the models is unnecessary here. However, for comparison with the present work, a brief over-all outline and summary is desirable.

The essence of these models might be captured as follows: Write the short-run production function of the form

$$Q_t = A N_t^\gamma h_t^\beta,$$

where Q_t is output in period t, N_t is the number of workers employed in period t, h_t is a labor utilization rate during the period (hours per man), and A is a constant (also possibly a function of time itself, and which includes all factors that are fixed in the short run, such as physical capital). The output elasticities, γ and β, are assumed constant over the sample period. Given a value of Q and a function of h, $w(h)$, that describes how wage rates vary with hours per head, the desired levels of N and h can be solved as a standard problem in cost minimization if, in fact, employment can be changed at no cost and without delay. Let N^* and h^* denote desired quantities. For example, on the Cobb-Douglas specification above, minimization of costs implies (assuming a constant wage)

$$N_t^* = Q^{1/\gamma} w^{a_1} e^{a_2 t}.$$

where the multiplicative constant term has been ignored, and a_1 and a_2 are constants. Desired labor stock is proportional to $Q^{1/\gamma}$, with adjustments for variations in the wage rate and for trend, the latter reflecting secular growth of capital and technical change. Then

$$\partial(\ln N)/\partial(\ln Q) = 1/\gamma.$$

On the basis of standard conditions on production functions, it must surely be the case that $\gamma < 1$, for otherwise the marginal product of labor would not decrease with N in the production function and the law of diminishing returns would be violated. Hence, in the short run, a change of one percentage point in output must lead to a change of more than one percentage point in labor stock employed. However, the empirical patterns described above clearly contradict this prediction: When output is rising relative to its trend, labor input does not rise by as much, and when output is falling relative to its trend, labor does not fall by as much. Therefore, at face value, such changes would imply a crude estimate of γ that is greater than unity, or estimated increasing returns to labor in the short run, in contradiction to the accepted theory of the firm.

Recognizing that costs of changing labor might be significant in layoff and hiring decisions, most investigators specify a stock adjustment hypothesis of which the following is an example:

$$N_t/N_{t-1} = (N_t^*/N_{t-1})^\lambda,$$

with $0 \leq \lambda < 1$ representing the adjustment coefficient in proportional terms. This allows for gradual adjustment of labor stock to its long-run desired value, rather than for instantaneous adjustment. As we shall observe in section D of this chapter, such a hypothesis implies a corresponding adjustment for utilization rates in order to meet the output and production function constraints during the adjustment period.

Substituting the variables determining N^* above into the adjustment hypothesis yields a regression model in which (with all variables other than trend measured in natural logarithms) current employment is regressed on output, wage rates, trend, and lagged employment. Some writers also employ an expectational notation for output rather than output itself; this involves adding lag terms in output to the regression equation. One investigation also allows for vintage effects in the production function, specifying the augmenting effects of new investment on labor productivity by including lagged investment terms in the regression equation as well as the other variables [Dhrymes, 1969]. Thus, the empirical model is of the form

$$\ln N_t = b_0 + b_1 \ln Q_t + b_2 \ln N_{t-1} + \text{other variables},$$

where the "other variables" include all the modifications used in the various specifications. Coefficient b_1 is an estimate of short-run labor-output elasticity; the estimated value $b_1/(1-b_2)$ is identified with $1/\gamma$, or the inverse of the output elasticity of labor stock in the short-run production function. Though estimates of this parameter $(1/\gamma)$ vary from study to study, depending on the precise specification, in most of them, γ is found to be greater than unity, implying increasing returns to labor alone. No really acceptable explanation of this result has yet been provided. Moreover, in most studies, exceptionally long adjustment lags to labor alone (i.e., values of b_2 near unity) have been found, so long, in fact, as to throw doubt on the assumption of fixed capital stock for purposes of "short-run" labor decisions.

One possible explanation for these estimates relates to a very complex adjustment process and the existence of lags elsewhere in the system. If one really takes the input-output production function constraint seriously, there is a real possibility that observed long adjustment delays of labor inputs may be only "sympathetic" reflections of long lags of other inputs, such as capital. Thus, if capital stock is the ultimate source of adjustment delay, all other inputs will reflect those long lags as a matter of course, so that output and sales are maintained over the adjustment period. The small adjustment coefficients estimated in most time-series employment models (i.e., large values of b_2) may not only reflect costly labor adjustments alone, but other adjustment costs as well. Therefore, they have no ready interpretation.

In other words, adjustment lags among inputs may not be independent. Indeed, the main contribution of this study is to specify and estimate interdependent factor demand functions that show distributed lag responses to be systematically time interrelated.

Finally, in a complete dynamic model, all inputs are changing. In such a model, the conditions underlying "short-run" input demand functions can be approximated by conceptual experiments in which some factors are considered "fixed" in the short run. Results of such experiments are reported in Chapter 7 and suggest that increasing returns to labor as estimated from time-series employment studies are due to omission of certain variables such as utilization rates. Large estimates of γ in those investigations should not be considered as returns to labor alone, but are more properly interpreted as short-run returns to both employment *and* capital utilization. Thus, our specification may help resolve an important issue that has arisen in the employment function literature.

C. INVESTMENT MODELS

The theoretical and empirical research on determinants of investment in fixed capital is voluminous and controversial. This is not the place for an in-depth survey and critique of all the issues involved. Therefore, only a narrow range of issues related to the recent quarterly time-series econometric models of investment behavior in U.S. manufacturing industries is summarized below. There are useful detailed surveys of the broader issues and estimates in articles by Eisner-Strotz [1963], Jorgenson-Hunter-Nadiri [1970], and Nadiri [1970]. Nerlove [1967] has also discussed, in a different context, some theoretical aspects of investment modeling.

Perhaps the most important issues discussed in the literature on fixed investment relate to (i) output and interest elasticity of investment; (ii) specification of the correct price of capital services; and (iii) distributed lag properties of capital stock adjustment. There are, of course, many other issues that deserve consideration, but we shall confine our discussion to these topics.

i. Output and Interest Elasticities

Investment functions of an earlier vintage, or those developed by, for example, Eisner [1960], Klein [1951], Meyer and Kuh [1957], and many others, were mainly of the stock adjustment type, in which the acceleration principle was combined with some measures of profitability. Distributed lag concepts of output as a measure of expected or "permanent" sales were often used, especially by Eisner. Others, like Duesenberry [1958] and Meyer and Kuh, included financial variables as measures of risk and profitability in addition to output.

Attempts to incorporate the interest rate as a determinant of investment behavior were unsuccessful because of several statistical and conceptual problems: high multicollinearity among the variables, difficulties in specifying the lag relation between interest rates and investment decisions, the general problem of specifying expectations, and possibly improper identification of interest rates as the rental price of capital (Jorgenson [1963]). In many empirical estimates, the output variables dominated all other kinds, especially the interest rate, leading to the view that investment demand was interest-inelastic.

Meyer and Kuh argued that the investment function is essentially nonlinear; that it differs in various phases of the business cycle, with sales being the dominant exogenous factor in the expansion phase of the cycle, and liquidity factors in the contraction phase. This characterization of investment behavior was further refined by the work of Meyer and Glauber [1964], using quarterly time-series data. Approaching the problem from a different vantage point, Anderson [1964] argued that balance sheet items such as debt-asset ratios and liquidity measures representing risk and portfolio adjustment considerations affect investment behavior. A more fully specified model of interdependent decisions between financial variables and investment in fixed capital has been estimated by Dhrymes and Kurz [1964] using firm data.

Differences in measurement of the variables and absence of comparability of basic data used in these studies make it very difficult to summarize all the empirical results. The general impression one gets from reading them is that the output variable is probably the most significant determinant of investment behavior, while financial variables may also influence investment behavior, albeit with small effect, except possibly in recession periods.

ii. The Neoclassical Model of Investment

Most of the recent discussion in the literature on investment behavior has been stimulated by the pioneering work of Jorgenson and associates (Jorgenson [1963], Jorgenson and Siebert [1968], Jorgenson and Stephenson [1967]). Jorgenson's argument is that substitution parameters have been improperly neglected or ignored in most work on investment behavior. He accepts the widely held specification that demand for capital is a function of output produced, but argues that it is also a function of the relative price of output and capital. Investment itself, then, consists of replacement of depreciating capital and distributed lag adjustment of capital to its equilibrium. Though Jorgenson suggests that, in quarterly data at least, a particular generalization of the techniques used by Chenery and Koyck for estimating distributed lag relations is essential, that question remains open ended.

In this work, the importance of factor prices, especially the cost of capital, is emphasized. Jorgenson points out that the correct measure of cost of capital services is an implicit rental or flow price, taking account of taxes, interest, depreciation, and capital gains or losses over the adjustment period. The empirical formulation of his models contains such measures (excluding capital gains, which may involve specification error in an inflationary economy), and adds distributed lag adjustments to an essentially long-run equilibrium model. Lags are rationalized in terms of institutionally determined states of investment-planning completion (Jorgenson [1963]). The empirical results reported by Jorgenson and associates based on quarterly postwar time-series data for manufacturing industries suggest the following:[1]

a. Investment demand is highly responsive to changes in relative prices, which include policy variables such as the interest rate and taxes.

b. The distributed lag response of investment to changes in its determinants is fairly long, about eight to nine quarters on the average, and there is no response in the first few quarters.

c. The distributed lag structure of investment behavior in each industry has a bell-like shape, implying that gross investment increases at an increasing rate in the short run and then increases at decreasing rates as long-run equilibrium is approached.

These conclusions, however, have recently been questioned. The controversy centers on the technological assumption of a Cobb-Douglas production function and the distributed lag specification of the model. The main issue concerning technology is whether or not the elasticity of investment with respect to relative prices equals unity. If the Cobb-Douglas production function is assumed, then the hypothesis of unitary elasticity of investment follows as a necessary consequence. Eisner and Nadiri [1968], on the assumption of a CES (constant elasticity of substitution) production function and data used by Jorgenson, show that the output elasticity of investment seems to be high—close to unity—and that its price elasticity is very low. This result was recently confirmed by Mayor [1971].

Jorgenson develops a sophisticated rational distributed lag mechanism, which is then added to "an essentially static theory of demand for capital services" (Nerlove [1971]). The lag distribution is interpreted as an unforeseen delivery lag, that is, firms can adjust their capital stock instantaneously but are prevented from realizing the optimal stock because of suppliers' delivery lags. Thus, it can be argued that, like most other investment functions, Jorgenson's model does not explicitly in-

1. The basic Jorgenson model has also been applied to time-series firm data (Jorgenson and Siebert [1968]) and public utility data (Jorgenson and Handel [1971]).

corporate the adjustment hypothesis as an integral part of the dynamic theory of capital accumulation (Nerlove [1971]).

What emerges from these discussions is that the role of price elasticity of investment and its distributed lag properties are unsettled questions. The magnitude of the price response depends on how the rental price is measured, what type of data are used, what sample period is used, what seasonal adjustment procedures are applied, what splicing techniques are used, how aggregated the data are, etc. The nature of the lag structure of investment behavior is an active area of theoretical research in the context of the models that explicitly account for adjustment costs.

With the possible exception of some of Jorgenson's writings, there is very little treatment of macromarket models in the literature. Most writers dealing with adjustment cost models concentrate on micro behavior and ignore the repercussions of these decisions on the capital goods market and the valuation of capital. It is implicitly assumed that the unit price of capital goods is fixed. Such an assumption would be tenable only in the unlikely event that the supply of investment goods (regardless of length of "run") were perfectly elastic. In all other cases, exogenous disturbances that affect the profitability of firms must generate changes in capital values, at least over some short intervals of time, and these are bound to influence actual behavior. Though Jorgenson does stress the inclusion of capital gains and losses in his (ideal) measure of implicit prices of capital services, the term is ignored in the empirical implementation of his model.

The study of investment behavior has been revolutionized in recent years by the direct integration of dynamic adjustment costs into the theory of the firm, as opposed to the simple grafting of a dynamic adjustment hypothesis such as (1.1) onto an essentially static theory. In a remarkable paper, Eisner and Strotz [1963] demonstrated that the flexible accelerator model actually could be derived directly from first principles of optimum accumulation. In their model, investment costs were specified as a quadratic function of the rate of investment. Thus, firms would not find it profitable to adjust instantaneously to long-run equilibrium, because of the increasing marginal costs of doing so. Instead, they would find it optimal to adjust slowly and distribute the adjustment costs over time, as shown by (1.1). This model was generalized, by Lucas [1967], Gould [1968], Treadway [1966], and Chetty and Sankar [1967], to include several factors of production. By examining approximations to first-order conditions along the paths of optimum accumulation, they derived generalized flexible accelerator models. Little empirical analysis along these lines has been reported, except by Schramm [1970], who assumed quadratic profit and cost functions.

Though the question of price expectations was seldom considered very crucial in the original versions of the accelerator model, the introduction of adjustment costs into the firm's decisions at the outset makes it imperative to treat both the expectations and the optimizing problem. In deriving flexible accelerators for the firm, most authors assume static price expectations. Gould [1968] has shown that under the more reasonable assumption of nonstatic price expectations current decisions depend on the entire future course of prices, and that characterization of optimum paths by flexible accelerator approximation is not generally possible.

In this work, we attempt to take account explicitly of adjustment costs of several inputs together, and jointly estimate an entire set of input demand functions that are mutually consistent and generated by a unified underlying structure. Before turning to a detailed examination of the model, we will illustrate with a simple example the nature of dynamic interactions among time paths of inputs and set up the more general discussion that will follow. We hope to demonstrate that the model provides a rationale for the high estimated output elasticity of labor input. It also provides new evidence on the price and output elasticity of investment and on their distributed lag properties.

D. AN EXAMPLE

Suppose the production function is $x = f(y_1, y_2)$, where x is output and the y_i ($i = 1, 2$) are inputs, with f displaying the usual continuity properties. Two isoquants are illustrated in Figure 1.1. The points A and B, derived in the usual way, represent efficient input combinations at which total costs are minimized. Though this may be an adequate description of long-run behavior, there is plenty of evidence to suggest that firms do not remain at points such as A and B at every moment of time. Since it is assumed that the changing of input levels is costly, some kind of partial adjustment model is called for. The conventional way of incorporating such lags is the partial adjustment model (1.1).

Suppose that for some reason the firm desires to increase output in Figure 1.1 from x_1 to x_2, given initial condition A. Then if factor prices are defined correctly, the long-run target or stationary values of the inputs (y_1^*, y_2^*), are given by point B. Consider the partial adjustment

FIGURE 1.1

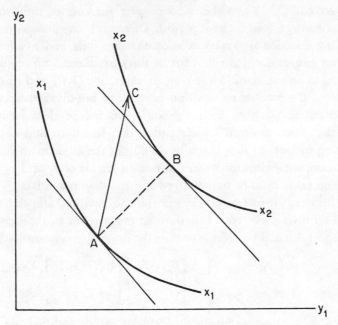

mechanism for input y_1:

$$y_{1t} - y_{1t-1} = \beta(y_1^* - y_{t-1}). \qquad (1.1')$$

Equation (1.1') implies an immediate move from A to (say) C, with convergence along isoquant x_2 to the new stationary point B. Therefore, given the production function and hypothesis (1.1'), an adjustment path for y_2 is *automatically implied*.

To illustrate, suppose f is Cobb-Douglas, i.e., $x = A y_1^a y_2^b$. Taking logs and rearranging,

$$\ln y_{2t} = -\frac{1}{b}\ln A + \frac{1}{b}\ln x_t - \frac{a}{b}\ln y_{1t}.$$

Using a log-linear form of (1.1'), $\ln(y_{1t}/y_{1t-1}) = \beta \ln(y_1^*/y_{1t-1})$ and substituting for y_{1t} in the expression above:

$$\ln y_{2t} = \frac{1}{b}\ln x_t - \frac{a}{b}\left[\beta \ln y_1^* + (1-\beta)\ln y_{1t-1}\right] - \frac{1}{b}\ln A$$

$$= \frac{1}{b}\ln x_t - \frac{a}{b}\beta \ln y_1^* - a\frac{(1-\beta)}{b}\ln y_{1t-1} - \frac{1}{b}\ln A.$$

The costs of increasing "hours per man" are the wages that must be paid existing employees to work the additional hour ($Y_1 w_p$ and $Y_6 w_n$) at the original wage per hour plus a correction for the fact that wage rates rise when hours are increased [$Y_1 Y_2 (dw_p/dY_2)$ and $Y_6 Y_7 (dw_n/dY_7)$]. Marginal factor cost of capital stock (Y_3) and intermediate product (Y_5) are simply c and c_I, respectively, while marginal factor cost c' at the capital-intensive margin is $p_k Y_3 (d\delta/dY_4)$, reflecting the increase in depreciation charges on capital stock when utilization is increased. The solution to the necessary conditions defines input demand functions, which are log-linear under the Cobb-Douglas assumption and given by the equation on the next page, where $k_1, k_2, \ldots, k_7$ are constants, parametric on $(Y_2/w_p)w_p'$, $(Y_7/w_n)w_n'$, $\alpha_1, \alpha_2, \ldots, \alpha_7$ and A (and therefore effects of trend via technical change are incorporated in the constants and not written explicitly in this formula). Also $\gamma = \alpha_1 + \alpha_3 + \alpha_5 + \alpha_6$. The factor demand functions may be written in more compact matrix notation as

$$Y^* = k + \xi Q + BR, \qquad (2.2)$$

where Y^* is a column vector of $\ln Y_i^*$ terms, ξ is a vector of scale effects, B is a matrix of factor price effects, and R is a vector of factor prices. It is apparent from the explicit form of (2.2) that the sum of elements in each row of B is zero. Hence, B is singular, expressing the fact that factor demand functions are homogeneous of degree zero in prices and that demand functions could be expressed equally as well in terms of price ratios.

There are several interesting properties of these solutions:

a. All long-run scale effects are embedded in stock demand functions and not in service flows per unit of stock, since output enters only the demand for stocks ($Y_1, Y_3, Y_5,$ and Y_6), not the demand for utilization rates ($Y_2, Y_4,$ and Y_7). For example, if output doubles and there are constant returns to scale then $\gamma = \alpha_1 + \alpha_3 + \alpha_5 + \alpha_6 = 1$, and all stock variables double, but hours per man and utilization of capital remain unchanged. This is clearly a desirable property of the solutions in view of casual observations we have made of the data. For example, hours per man and the amount of shift working have remained reasonably constant on the average during the post-World War II period of our data (see Chapter 3) in spite of massive secular changes in real output. Utilization rates display considerable variation over the sample period, but these are mainly short-run phenomena, independent of the long-run considerations under

MODEL (2.2)

$$
\begin{bmatrix} \ln w_p \\ \ln s_p \\ \ln c \\ \ln c' \\ \ln c_I \\ \ln w_n \\ \ln s_n \end{bmatrix}
\begin{bmatrix}
\dfrac{\alpha_6-\alpha_7}{\gamma} & \dfrac{\alpha_7}{\gamma} & \dfrac{\alpha_5}{\gamma} & \dfrac{\alpha_4}{\gamma} & \dfrac{\alpha_3-\alpha_4}{\gamma} & \dfrac{\alpha_1-\alpha_2}{\gamma}-1 & \dfrac{\alpha_2}{\gamma} \\[2ex]
0 & 0 & 0 & 0 & 0 & +1 & -1 \\[2ex]
\dfrac{\alpha_6-\alpha_7}{\gamma} & \dfrac{\alpha_7}{\gamma} & \dfrac{\alpha_5}{\gamma} & \dfrac{\alpha_4}{\gamma} & \dfrac{\alpha_3-\alpha_4}{\gamma}-1 & \dfrac{\alpha_1-\alpha_2}{\gamma} & \dfrac{\alpha_2}{\gamma} \\[2ex]
0 & 0 & 0 & -1 & +1 & 0 & 0 \\[2ex]
\dfrac{\alpha_6-\alpha_7}{\gamma} & \dfrac{\alpha_7}{\gamma} & \dfrac{\alpha_5}{\gamma}-1 & \dfrac{\alpha_4}{\gamma} & \dfrac{\alpha_3-\alpha_4}{\gamma} & \dfrac{\alpha_1-\alpha_2}{\gamma} & \dfrac{\alpha_2}{\gamma} \\[2ex]
\dfrac{\alpha_6-\alpha_7}{\gamma}-1 & \dfrac{\alpha_7}{\gamma} & \dfrac{\alpha_5}{\gamma} & \dfrac{\alpha_4}{\gamma} & \dfrac{\alpha_3-\alpha_4}{\gamma} & \dfrac{\alpha_1-\alpha_2}{\gamma} & \dfrac{\alpha_2}{\gamma} \\[2ex]
+1 & -1 & 0 & 0 & 0 & 0 & 0
\end{bmatrix}
\begin{bmatrix} \dfrac{1}{\gamma} \\ 0 \\ \dfrac{1}{\gamma} \\ 0 \\ \dfrac{1}{\gamma} \\ \dfrac{1}{\gamma} \\ 0 \end{bmatrix}[\ln Q]
+ \begin{bmatrix} k_1 \\ k_2 \\ k_3 \\ k_4 \\ k_5 \\ k_6 \\ k_7 \end{bmatrix}
= \begin{bmatrix} \ln Y_1^* \\ \ln Y_2^* \\ \ln Y_3^* \\ \ln Y_4^* \\ \ln Y_5^* \\ \ln Y_6^* \\ \ln Y_7^* \end{bmatrix}
$$

discussion here. There are increasing, constant, or decreasing returns to scale in the conventional sense when $\gamma = \alpha_1 + \alpha_3 + \alpha_5 + \alpha_6$ is greater than, equal to, or less than unity.

Scale does not affect utilization rates in this formulation due to the nature of the assumed production function. Consider the marginal conditions for Y_1 and Y_2, $MFC_1/MFC_2 = MP_1/MP_2$. On Cobb-Douglas assumptions we have

$$\frac{w_p Y_2 + s_p}{Y_1(w_p + Y_2 w_p')} = (\alpha_1/\alpha_2)\,(Y_2/Y_1),$$

and Y_1 enters the denominator of both sides and cancels out, leaving an expression determining Y_2 independently of all other variables. If the elasticity of substitution between Y_1 and Y_2 were not unity, then it would not necessarily be true that utilization rate demand functions would be scale-free. Finally, if $F(Y_1, \ldots, Y_7)$ were not homogeneous, scale effects would not be the same in all stock equations, as they are in the Cobb-Douglas formulation.

b. Factor prices affect long-run input demand functions in various ways, which differ from the familiar solutions. Most surprisingly, a relative increase in hourly wage rates increases demand for labor stocks Y_1 or Y_6. However, it decreases demand for labor utilization, Y_2 or Y_7. The reason is that an increase in w relative to s (given output) induces substitution of stock for utilization, since hours per man become relatively more expensive than numbers, pushing out the extensive margin relative to the intensive margin. However, the former effect is not as great as the latter, since an increase in w reduces total man-hours and increases capital services, as usual. For example,

$$\partial \ln (Y_1 Y_2) \,/\, \partial \ln w = \left(\frac{\alpha_2}{\gamma} - 1\right) < 0.$$

On the other hand, an increase in user costs (s_p or s_n) reduces demand for labor stocks, since they become relatively more expensive, and induces substitution of hours per man and capital stock to maintain output. Changes in w and s only affect capital (positively), but do not influence the rate of utilization of capital. Similarly, a relative increase in some component of c induces substitution of capital utilization for capital stock and increases employment without affecting hours per man. An increase in the cost of inventories, c_I, has a negative own effect, but a positive effect on all other stock variables, which does not affect any utilization rate. Again, these conclusions might be altered slightly in a more general formulation.

c. In setting up the problem as one of cost minimization, we concentrate on factor substitution and ignore price-induced scale effects. All relative factor price changes increase marginal cost of output and eventually lead to decreases in desired output, working toward reductions in all inputs. Thus, if the latter effect were to be included, an increase in w_p would increase Y_1 (labor stock) due to substitution, but decrease it due to scale. The net change depends on the magnitudes of both effects.

d. Long-run utilization rates are independent of cross-price effects. Thus, c and c_1 do not enter demand functions for Y_2 and Y_7 (labor utilization) nor do w_p, w_n, s_p, and s_n affect the demand for Y_4 (capital utilization). Such independence evidently is due to the assumption of Cobb-Douglas production functions and is not a general consequence of the theory for any production function. However, it is not obvious a priori how the theory predicts signs of cross effects on the usual general assumptions of production functions.

B. SHORT-RUN ADJUSTMENTS

As noted previously, there is no reason to expect firms to be in long-run equilibrium at every point in time. Therefore, time-series data reflect temporary and short-run influences that are not fully captured by any long-run model. Our brief review of the literature suggests that the most satisfactory empirical time-series specification postulates lagged adjustment to some "desired" targets, and we adopt a modified version of that hypothesis.

Specify a log-linear adjustment hypothesis (with all variables measured in natural logarithms):

$$Y_{it} - Y_{it-1} = \sum_{j=1}^{7} \beta_{ij}(Y_{jt}^* - Y_{jt-1}) + \varepsilon_{it}; \quad i = 1, \ldots, 7; \qquad (2.3)$$

where Y_{jt}^* is the desired or target level of input ($\ln Y_j$) in period t, defined by (2.2), ε_{it} is a random variable, and the β_{ij} are fixed adjustment coefficients. On specification (2.3), $Y_{jt}^* - Y_{jt-1}$ is the proportional divergence between actual and desired input levels at the start of the period under consideration, or relative "excess demand" (or "excess supply" if negative) for factor Y_j. The systematic portion of (2.3)—that is, excluding ε_{it}— asserts that the relative change in each input is proportional to the divergence between desired and actual levels of *all other* inputs as well as to its own level of excess demand. This specification introduces *feedbacks and interrelated adjustments among all factors of production.* For example, suppose that there exists excess demand for production workers (Y_1). If product demand has increased due to a business cycle expansion, disequilibrium in the stock of production workers is likely to call forth extraordinary adjustments in factors such as utilization rates that are more easily altered in the short run. Firms may well find it desirable to increase both hours of work (overtime) and capital utilization, both of which can be altered at less cost in the short run, in order to take up the slack of less than optimal labor stock. The equation system (2.3) is designed to capture all such effects on a symmetrical and internally consistent basis. To elaborate on these complex issues we need to consider the conceptual basis of adjustment processes, some qualifications to these arguments, and the nature of disturbances in the system. These issues are considered in what follows.

i. Costs of Adjustment: Theoretical Considerations

Note that system (2.3) can be derived for a firm from principles of wealth maximization across an infinite horizon, when changes in factors generate "costs of adjustment" (see Lucas [1967]) as mentioned in Chapter 1. Indeed, (2.3) is simply a generalization of the well-known flexible accelerator, or partial adjustment model, and it is appropriate at this point to review the principles underlying its derivation.

Consider a competitive firm selling a single good x, producing with a vector of n inputs y. Let μ be a vector of fixed "depreciation" rates, some of which may be zero; p is product price, and v is a vector of fixed input prices. Let $g(\dot{y}+\mu'y)$ be a function denoting costs of gross changes in inputs, or costs of adjustment, with $dy/dt = \dot{y}$. The function $g(\ )$ represents market search and training costs for such inputs as labor, and installation and "gestation" costs for inputs such as capital. Assume that $g(0) = 0$, and $g_i, g_{ii} > 0$ for $|\dot{y}+\mu y| \neq 0$, and that the derivatives do not change sign at the origin. Further, assume

$$\lim_{z_i \to 0} g_i(z) = 0 \quad \text{and} \quad \lim_{z_i \to \infty} g_i(z) = \infty.$$

Then the present value of the firm is

$$W = \int_0^\infty [px - vy - g(\dot{y} + \mu'y)]e^{-rt}\,dt, \tag{2.4}$$

where r is the rate of interest. Maximization of W, subject to the initial conditions, y_0, and the production function (2.1), $x = F(y)$, requires choosing a set of functions $y_i(t)$, describing optimum input levels at each point in time. Note that its solution requires knowledge of $p(t)$ and $v(t)$, the future course of prices over the horizon. Conditions for maximization of (2.4) are

$$pF_i - v_i = g_i[r + \mu_i - (\dot{g}_i/g_i)]; \quad i = 1, 2, \ldots, n;$$

$$\lim_{t \to \infty} g_i e^{-rt} = 0; \tag{2.5}$$

where F_i and g_i are derivatives of F and g with respect to their ith arguments. The first equation of (2.5) must hold at every point in the planning horizon and characterizes the optimum functions $y_i(t)$. In this formulation, marginal value products are not set equal to factor prices for maximization. Instead, marginal value products exceed factor prices by an amount that reflects costs of changing inputs along the optimal path. The term on the right-hand side of (2.5) is simply the marginal stock cost of adjusting inputs, amortized to a periodic flow. Note that this term is not constant along the optimum path, but varies, depending on the actual changes in y. The second equation in (2.5) is a condition guaranteeing that (2.4) has a finite maximum. Given the course of $p(t)$ and $v(t)$ over the horizon and the initial conditions, (2.5) is a simultaneous set of nonlinear differential equations in y. These may be solved for optimal paths of each input, $y_i(t)$, over time. The complete solution to (2.5) is in general very difficult to obtain, and most analyses proceed by linearizing the nonlinear terms F_i and g_i, which amounts to taking second-order or quadratic approximations to the production and cost functions (Eisner and Strotz [1963], Lucas [1967], and Schramm [1970]). Under certain conditions, the solution to the linearized form of (2.5) can be expressed in the form of the systematic portion of (2.3). A crucial condition for derivation of generalized flexible accelerators (2.3) is the constancy of p and w over the horizon (Gould [1968]), an assumption known as "static expectations." In such a case, the process (2.5) converges to the equilibrium

$$pF_i = v_i + \bar{g}_i(r + \mu_i); \quad i = 1, 2, \ldots, n; \tag{2.6}$$

where $\bar{g}_i$ is g_i evaluated at $\mu'\bar{y}$, and $\bar{y}$ is the equilibrium value of y.[3]

---

3. A more general formulation of total costs is $g(y, \dot{y} + \mu'y)$. In (24.), $g_{12} = 0$ since terms in y and $\dot{y} + \mu'y$ are independent. If $g_{12} \neq 0$, and adjustment costs are nonseparable,

Conditions (2.6) are in fact the usual ones for maximum profit under static conditions, namely, that marginal value product equals marginal factor cost. Indeed, the simultaneous solution of (2.6) yields y_i as functions of p and v_i, and these functions define the desired *fixed* targets y_i^* in (2.3) and, in fact, are similar to our equation (2.2). At that point, the firm must be minimizing costs, and an equivalent set of targets can be found by specifying the ordinary factor demand functions [such as (2.2) in section A above] at the stationary value of output that is consistent with the solution to (2.6). Finally, the adjustment coefficients β_{ij} are clearly related to the properties of $g(\dot{y} + \mu y)$. In cases where p and v are not constant, the particular solutions to (2.5) depend on the explicit evolution of prices, and flexible accelerator formulations do not necessarily apply. The reason is apparent from the specification of fixed targets in (2.3). Evidently, the fixed targets arise because p and w are fixed. If p and w are not constant, the targets at which the firm aims undergo change, and (2.3) cannot hold.

ii. Some Qualifications

It is important to point out that the data to be analyzed are generated by *markets* and are aggregate in character. Therefore, micromodels of the firm are not testable in the absence of consideration of market repercussions on firm behavior. In particular, the assumption of static expectations is not tenable when one considers market feedbacks. Consider a unit once-and-for-all shock in the market demand function for output in a competitive industry. Market price, p, immediately rises, since short-run supply is inelastic. If we now attempt to reason along the lines of the model above for a "representative" firm, it will turn out that static price expectations are unrealized at every point in time. Actual price will always turn out to be lower than expected price as industry output rises and price falls along the new demand schedule. Ex post, firm output decisions during the adjustment period will have been too high, and in that sense nonoptimal. In the face of such losses, it is probable that learning will occur, and firms will begin to anticipate market reactions more or less correctly. If so, such anticipations by all firms will, in themselves, have repercussions on market prices as all firms react and short-run supply is affected.

---

some of the conclusions in the text are slightly altered. For a discussion of this issue see Treadway [1966] and Nerlove [1971].

Perhaps a concept such as "rational expectations" (Muth [1960]) is appropriate here. But in any event, p cannot be considered as constant over the adjustment period. In addition, it may even be true that attempts by all firms to expand will have repercussions on the price of inputs. Even if wages remain fixed, capital goods prices must certainly change. Firms have access to capital goods either by purchasing other firms or by ordering new equipment from capital goods producers and these supplies are not perfectly elastic. Therefore, the fixed targets hypothesis of cost-adjustment models is untenable in a market setting.

In view of these limitations of cost-adjustment models of the firm for market behavior, some modifications are necessary. Our modifications take the form of retaining the highly suggestive lag specification of (2.3). However, the target and disturbance terms are altered in a manner that captures some of the *industry* variation in factor demand. In particular, we relax the specification of *fixed* targets toward which the system moves.

Our basic view is that there exists *short-run* monopoly power in product and factor markets; that is, during the adjustment process, firms do not regard product and factor prices as fixed parameters, at which they can sell or buy all conceivable quantities of output and inputs, but in fact, exercise some control over their prices. It is only in the long run, under conditions of reasonable stability, that the forces of potential and actual entry and exit of firms force the stringent conditions of competition on markets (Arrow [1959]). The empirical evidence for this view is well known and can be briefly stated. Prices vary, but simply do not fall by as much as might be expected during recessions and do not rise by as much as might be expected during recovery periods (Stigler and Kindahl [1970]). Indeed, money wage rates have hardly fallen at all during the entire postwar period (see Chart 3.8). Since resources cannot move freely in and out of industries in the face of "adjustment costs" and uncertainty about the future, firms must take account of the future reactions of the market and, thereby, of other firms in making their current decisions. This in itself is sufficient to produce a kind of short-run imperfection in the market.[4]

The upshot of this hypothesis is that desired or target factor demands are not wholly a function of current product and factor prices. Instead, the representative firm exercises some of its short-run control, depending

4. Formal models along these lines are given in Phelps [1970].

on the type and extent of disturbances in the market, by stabilizing prices and thereby fixing output, input, and inventory targets.

iii. *Characterization of Disturbances*

More specifically, (2.3) represents dynamic responses of inputs whose precise movements depend on "shocks" to the system. As noted above, these shocks can best be analyzed in terms of final demand or *sales*. So far, it has been assumed that additions to finished goods inventories are part of current output. Sales, output, and additions to inventories of finished goods are related by the identity $S_t + \Delta I_t = Q_t$, where S is the level of sales and ΔI_t is output inventory investment. If it is true that disturbances arise from fluctuations in the demand for final goods and that marginal production cost is increasing, firms will meet part of their final demand from stocks of finished inventory. This suggests a sales "production function," $S_t = f(Q_t, I_t)$, that allows for the holding of buffer stocks and production smoothing (Lovell [1969]; Holt et al. [1960]). Therefore we may write as an approximation:

$$S_t = H(Y_{it}); \quad i = 1, \ldots, 7;$$

where all Y_i's are defined as in section A, above, except for Y_5, which now refers to total inventories of both finished and unfinished goods. Thus, total inventory is a decision variable in the model.[5]

It is useful to make a distinction between what are regarded as "permanent" changes and those that are regarded as "temporary" shocks. Such analysis has proven useful in a wide variety of time-series models and may have some payoff for the problem at hand (Eisner [1967] and Friedman [1957]). Accordingly, let $Y_j^* = Y_{jt}^P + Y_{jt}^T$, where Y_{jt}^P is the permanent component, and Y_{jt}^T is the transitory component of the target level of input j. Y_{jt}^P is meant to capture all secular long-run forces that drive the system and that are clearly foreseen by firms. These forces result from growth in the economy in general; secularly increasing demand for industry output, such as population growth; technical change

---

5. Strictly speaking, inventory decision models are most meaningful in the presence of uncertainty, where prices and sales are random variables (Arrow, Karlin, and Scarf [1958]; Zabel [1967]). We have adopted the present method in order to introduce finished goods inventory into an essentially deterministic system. However, stochastic elements are introduced in the manner discussed below. Marketing and advertising costs might be included, too, but we have not done so.

in the economy; and general capital accumulation. For the most part, Y_{jt}^p is to be identified with trend. However, it may also include nontrend extrapolations based on some kind of long-term smoothed average of past experience. This hypothesis suggests that Q_t in expression (2.2) above should be regarded as S_t^p, an unobserved target level of sales that would be maintained under competitive market conditions in a long period of relative stability (Nerlove [1967a]). That is, we envision a relatively fixed long-run supply function in the industry (possibly increasing with respect to price, possibly not) and a demand function that is rising at a rather steady rate, with superimposed disturbances. The long-run rate of growth of demand depends largely on economic growth in general and on the income elasticity of demand for the product in particular.

To see what this entails, suppose there were no random shocks in the economy. Assuming system (2.3) to be stable, it will eventually "damp" down to a long-run equilibrium trend. If the initial conditions are not along the trend line, all inputs converge to their long-run rates of growth (possibly zero, as with Y_2), which in general equals the rate of growth of sales, corrected for returns to scale and technological changes in production of the given industry. Long-run factor proportions will depend on prices, as usual. In such a case, S_t^p will eventually become the observed S_t, rather than an unobserved component, if the data are available for a sufficiently long period of time.

Evidently, long-run trends are not the only forces moving the system. There are transitory shocks as well. In this regard, it is useful to distinguish two types of disturbances. The first are purely random shocks that are strictly uncorrelated with each other over time. Since this is the usual econometric specification, no further elaboration is necessary.

The second, and for present purposes more interesting, type of disturbances that shock the system is identified with certain types of business cycle activity around the long-run trend. It is here that our distinction between short-run monopoly power and long-run competitiveness comes into play. It is clear that since business cycle activity displays substantial serial correlation, some of its components are regular enough to be in part predictable on the basis of past observations. Firms attempt to maintain short-run sales targets on the basis of such predictions. Thus, we specify short-run deviations from the long-run targets based on short-run monopoly power in the product market, as part of the desired target, Y_t^*. As an empirical proposition, and in the face of sticky product prices, these are taken to be related to predicted sales during transitional periods. As will be discussed in detail below, short-run sales targets are specified functions of past observations, new orders, back orders, and so on. Thus, in the relevant "long run" (never observed), the expected values of the short-run deviations from long-run trend targets are zero.

In sum, our specification is: (a) equation (2.3), allowing interactions and feedbacks between factor demand functions; (b) specification (2.2) for the moving long-run target variables in Y_t^*, with S^P replacing output and representing an unobserved "permanent" component of sales closely associated with trend; and (c) an additional specification for short-term deviations in these targets, depending on predicted sales in the immediate future. The model is (in matrix notation):

$$Y_t = \beta Y_t^* + (I - \beta)\, Y_{t-1} + \varepsilon_{1t}; \qquad \text{(a)}$$

$$Y_t^* = Y_t^P + Y_t^T; \qquad \text{(b)}$$

$$Y_t^P = k + \rho S_t^P + BR_t + \varepsilon_{2t}; \qquad \text{(c)}$$

$$Y_t^T = \varphi(Z_t - S_t^P) + \varepsilon_{3t}. \qquad \text{(d)}$$

(2.7)

All variables are in logarithms: β is the matrix of adjustment coefficients, $\{\beta_{ij}\}$, and I is the identity matrix. The vector of inputs at time t is Y_t, and Y_t^* is the vector of desired target levels of inputs at time t. The second relation partitions targets into permanent and transitory components, as above. In the third relation, Y^P is specified to be a vector of log-linear functions, as in equation (2.2), that depend on the permanent component of sales, S_t^P, and a vector of factor prices R_t. In the empirical work, the singularity restriction on the price response matrix B is imposed by using price ratios in R_t, rather than their absolute level. ρ is a vector of long-run sales elasticities of each input. The fourth relationship specifies the cyclical and temporary but systematic shocks that drive the system, Y_t^T, as linear functions of the difference between predicted sales during transitional periods, Z_t, and the permanent components. φ is a vector of constants. The precise content of Z_t is a matter of empirical judgment, and discussion of it is deferred to a later chapter. Finally, the ε terms are vectors of unsystematic, serially uncorrelated random disturbances, with zero means and finite variances. The hypothesis of time independence is maintained for these variables. Of course, contemporaneous disturbances may, in fact, be correlated across equations, that is, ε_{ijt} and ε_{klt} do not necessarily exhibit zero covariance.

C. RESTRICTIONS ON ADJUSTMENT COEFFICIENTS

On our interpretation of short-run adjustment mechanisms, firms maintain their position along the production surface at every point in time; that is, firms are not "off" their production functions during the adjustment process. Note that this does not mean that such phenomena as labor "hoarding" or temporary excess capacity are not possible, for utilization rates can vary in an opposite way. Moreover, the essence of the adjustment mechanism in (2.7) is that excess demands or supplies of factors "held" by firms exist during the adjustment period. Imposition of production function constraints means that if some excess demands exist, some excess supplies must exist as well, in order to maintain output.

Some examples will clarify the point. Suppose a recession occurs. If changes are so rapid that they are not perfectly foreseen by all firms, it is reasonable to suppose that holdings of capital stock at current rates of output and sales will be greater than would be desirable under stationary conditions at recession rates of output. In this sense there would be excess holdings of capital stock. But the productive capacity of capital depends not only on stock magnitudes, but also on rates of stock utilization. Thus, in the present case, capital utilization declines, producing the recession-induced lower rates of output (this discussion ignores production for inventory). In a similar vein, suppose the firm finds itself in the position of carrying "excess" workers on its payroll, or of hoarding employees. Then, if it were possible properly to measure utilization or intensity of work of these employees, use of a measure of real input would result in a measure of actual current output.

On the basis of these examples, certain relationships between the adjustment coefficients β_{ij} in (2.3) or (2.7) are implied by the constraint. This was also illustrated in the example of Chapter 1, and can be analyzed by considering equation (2.7a) in detail. Repeating it for convenience,

$$Y_t = \beta Y_t^* + (I - \beta) Y_{t-1} + \varepsilon_t. \tag{2.7a}$$

In addition, assume the sales production function can be approximated by[6] $S_t = \alpha' Y_t$, where α' is a vector of constants ("sales elasticities" for each component of Y). Substituting the adjustment hypothesis (2.7a) into

---

6. The need for approximation here arises because sales, output, and inventory changes are linearly related, whereas, on Cobb-Douglas assumptions, output and inputs are related in a log-linear fashion.

the sales production function yield s

$$S_t = \alpha'\beta Y_t^* + \alpha' (I - \beta) Y_{t-1}.$$

Now, consider the condition

$$\alpha'(I - \beta) = 0, \tag{2.8}$$

or, equivalently, $\alpha'I = \alpha'\beta$, implying certain restrictions on possible values of β_{ij}. Equation (2.8) is in fact a set of n equations relating α_j and β_{ij}. By the equality in the sentence above, it is seen to amount to the condition

$$\sum_j \alpha_j \beta_{ij} = \alpha_i; \ i = 1, \ldots, n;$$

that is, a weighted column sum (over j) of β_{ij}, with weights equal to the sales elasticities, must sum to the appropriate sales elasticity itself. Evidently, since the terms in α_j are all nonzero (otherwise, input j would not be a proper input), equation (2.8) implies that matrix $(I - \beta)$ is singular, or that $|I - \beta| = 0$. It also implies that all elements in any row of $(I - \beta)$ cannot be of the same sign. That is, inputs must react positively to excess demands for some Y_i's and negatively to excess demands for others. In principle, $|I - \hat{\beta}| = 0$, where $\hat{\beta}$ is a matrix of estimated values, provides a test of the production function restriction. We emphasize "in principle" because sampling distributions of the roots of $|I - \hat{\beta}|$ are not readily available. However, these roots are computed as a matter of course in what follows, and the smallest root should give some indication of the restriction. Alternatively, the restrictions on β could be imposed on the estimation procedure at the outset. This alternative is considered in a later section. Notice that restriction (2.8) has an additional implication regarding S_t and Y_t^*. In particular, if (2.8) holds,

$$S_t = \alpha'\beta Y_t^* + \alpha'\varepsilon_t = \alpha'Y_t^* + \alpha'\varepsilon_t. \tag{2.9}$$

The expected value of a weighted sum of the target values of Y^* must equal sales. The meaning of this should be apparent from the discussion of Y^* itself. Recall that Y^* consists of two components: a long-run trend or permanent component Y^P and a short-run cyclical component, Y^T. The latter term reflects transitory deviations from long-run sales; the input targets resulting from cyclical fluctuations are due to short-run monopoly power exercised by firms. Condition (2.9) simply means that the target sales are in fact produced on the average, or that sales forecasts are realized on average. Thus, a component of Y^T changes in the short run to guarantee this to be so. If exogenous disturbances make it desirable for the firm to produce something other than S^p, then Y^T is nonzero to reflect that decision.

D. DYNAMIC PROPERTIES OF THE SYSTEM

Equations (2.7) may be called the structural specification of the model. It is useful to examine the implications of the reduced form to check on the consistency of the structure. In particular, all dynamic models can always be cast in the form of weighted sums of previous values and initial conditions by iteration.

To this end, consider the systematic portion of (2.7a) and assume some vector of initial inputs Y_0. Then by recursion, it follows that

$$Y_t = \beta Y_t^* + (I - \beta) \beta Y_{t-1}^* + \ldots + (I - \beta)^{t-1} Y_1^*$$
$$+ (I - \beta)^t Y_0, \quad (2.10)$$

and Y_t is a weighted sum of all past desired values, Y_t^*, and of the initial condition, Y_0. Analysis of (2.10) consists of a set of conceptual experiments designed to determine dynamic responses to various shocks.

Consider equilibrium properties first. For this purpose assume all values of Y_t^* are constant and equal over time: $Y_1^* = Y_2^* = Y_3^* = \ldots = Y^*$. Then equilibrium requires $Y_t = Y^*$. If the system runs for a sufficiently long period of time, there must come a point where actual values of Y_t settle arbitrarily near Y^* and remain there. Denote the equilibrium value of Y_t by $\overline{Y}$. Then, at equilibrium, $Y_t = Y_{t-1} = \overline{Y}$. Substituting into (2.7a), we have

$$\overline{Y} = \beta Y^* + (I - \beta) \overline{Y}$$

or

$$[I - (I - \beta)] \overline{Y} = \beta \overline{Y} = \beta Y^*$$

as required.

Next, consider the question of stability. Given equilibrium values of Y^* in our conceptual experiment, will the actual values of Y_t eventually converge to Y^* from any initial condition Y_0 if left to run for a sufficiently long period of time? The answer to this question can be obtained from (2.10). Setting $\{Y_t^*\} = \{Y^*\}$,

$$Y_t = [I + (I - \beta) + (I - \beta)^2 + \ldots + (I - \beta)^{t-1}]\beta Y^*$$
$$+ (I - \beta)^t Y_0. \quad (2.11)$$

Clearly, the convergence of this series depends on the properties of $(I - \beta)$. As is well known, stability requires $(I - \beta)^t$ to converge to the zero matrix as t approaches infinity. If that is true, then the matrix sum $[I + (I - \beta) + (I - \beta)^2 + \dots]$ converges to β^{-1}, from which it follows [from (2.11)], that, in the limit, Y_t approaches its equilibrium value, Y^*.

$(I - \beta)$ is similar to a diagonal matrix, $(I - \beta) = P\Lambda P^{-1}$, where Λ is a diagonal matrix of characteristic roots of $(I - \beta)$ and P is a square matrix.[7] Also,

$$(I - \beta)^m = (P\Lambda P^{-1})(P\Lambda P^{-1}) \dots (P\Lambda P^{-1}) = P\Lambda^m P^{-1}$$

Since Λ is diagonal, Λ^m can be expressed as the diagonal elements all raised to the power m. Therefore, as m increases $(I - \beta)^m$ approaches zero if each element of Λ approaches zero, requiring all characteristic roots to lie within the unit circle.

We now know the properties guaranteeing convergence to "equilibrium." An equally important question concerns the speed of response, or properties, of the approach to equilibrium. For this purpose, it is necessary to investigate transient responses of the system, defined as the response to a one-time unit impulse. Consider an initial equilibrium at which $Y_t = \bar{Y}$ and $Y_t^* = Y^*$ and $\bar{Y} = Y^*$. Denote

$$\tilde{Y}_t = Y_t - \bar{Y};$$
$$\tilde{Y}_t^* = Y_t^* - Y^*.$$

Then (2.7a) may be written

$$\tilde{Y}_t = \beta\tilde{Y}_t^* + (I - \beta)\tilde{Y}_{t-1}. \tag{2.12}$$

The transient response of the system is obtained by analyzing the conditions $\tilde{Y}_0 = 0$, $\tilde{Y}_1^* = 1$, $\tilde{Y}_2^* = \tilde{Y}_3^* = \dots = \tilde{Y}_m^* = \dots = 0$. Iterating (2.12) with these assumptions yields

$$\tilde{Y}_1 = \beta Y_1^* = \beta;$$
$$\tilde{Y}_2 = \beta(0) + (I - \beta)\tilde{Y}_1 = (I - \beta)\beta\tilde{Y}_1^* = (I - \beta)\beta; \tag{2.13}$$
$$\dots\dots\dots\dots$$
$$\tilde{Y}_t = (I - \beta)^{t-1}\beta.$$

7. The number of nonzero characteristic roots for Λ equals the rank of $(I - \beta)$. Thus, if the restrictions hold, we know that $(I - \beta)$ is singular and has rank $n - 1$. If they do not hold, it has rank n.

In this experiment, Y_t^* has been increased by unity in the first period and then reduced to its initial value thereafter. Conditions (2.13) show that the effects of this unit impulse are not confined to the first-period response, but are *distributed* over time. Thus, $\tilde{Y}_1$ is the first-period or impact response, $\tilde{Y}_2$ is the second-period response, and so on. From the general form of $\tilde{Y}_t$ in (2.13) stability properties of $(I - \beta)$ guarantee that the effects of the impulse gradually converge to zero. The (normalized) patterns of $\{\tilde{Y}_t\}$ in (2.13) are in fact equivalent to distributed lag patterns found in all lag models, as will be shown in a moment.

It is also interesting to investigate the response to a unit step-function impulse, or once-and-for-all-time shock to the system, rather than to a one-time unit shock. That is, let $Y_1^* = Y_2^* = \ldots = 1$. By the same reasoning as above, responses in each period are simply the sum of the distributed lag effects in (2.13):

$$\tilde{Y}_1 = \beta;$$

$$\tilde{Y}_2 = \beta + (I - \beta)\,\beta;$$

$$\cdots\cdots\cdots$$

$$\tilde{Y}_t = \beta + (I - \beta)\,\beta + (I - \beta)^2\beta + \ldots + (I - \beta)^{t-1}\beta;$$

which converges either to the step value, 1, itself, or to the new equilibrium level.

E. COMPARISON WITH OTHER MODELS: THEORETICAL CONSIDERATIONS

It is useful to rewrite the system in another way, to facilitate comparison with other models in the literature. "Partial" reduced form expressions may be obtained in which each dependent variable is expressed in terms of lagged desired targets, Y^*, and lagged own values, Y_{it-1}. To simplify the algebra, let L be the lag operator: $LY_t = Y_{t-1}$, $L^2Y_{t-1} = Y_{t-2}$, etc. In this notation, (2.7a) may be rewritten (ignoring stochastic terms) as $[I - (I - \beta)L]Y_t = \beta Y_t^*$, and an equivalent reduced form is

$$Y_t = [I - (I - \beta)\,L]^{-1}\beta Y_t^*. \tag{2.14}$$

Each element of $[I - (I - \beta)L]^{-1}$ is a rational polynomial function of L. In fact, each element is the ratio of two polynomial functions of the lag operator; the parameters depend on the particular values of β_{ij}. The denominator of each of these functions is the determinant $|I - (I - \beta)L|$, or a polynomial function of L, $\Theta(L)$,

$$\Theta(L) = b_0 (1 - b_1 L - b_2 L^2 - \ldots - b_m L^m),$$

where the coefficients $b_0, b_1, \ldots$ are functions of β_{ij}. In fact, m, the order of $\Theta(L)$, is $n - 1$ if the production function restrictions apply [$(I - \beta)$ is singular]. Otherwise, it is of order n. Similarly, the numerator of each term in the inverse matrix is another polynomial in L, $\Theta_{ij}(L)$, with

$$\Theta_{ij}(L) = a_{0j} + a_{1j} L + \ldots + a_{n-1j} L^{n-1}; \quad i = 1, \ldots, n-1;$$

where $a_{0j}, a_{1j}, \ldots$ are also functions of β_{ij}. The order of $\Theta_{ij}(L)$ is $n - 1$ irrespective of the production function restrictions. We have

$$[I - (I - \beta)L]^{-1} = \{\Theta_{ij}(L)\} / \Theta(L). \tag{2.15}$$

Carrying out the multiplication in (2.14) after substituting (2.15) yields

$$Y_{it} = \left[\sum_j \Theta_{ij}(L)\beta_{\cdot j} Y_{jt}^*\right] / \Theta(L); \quad i = 1, \ldots, n. \tag{2.16}$$

Finally, multiplying both sides of (2.16) by $\Theta(L)$ yields an equivalent distributed lag formulation,

$$Y_{it} = \frac{1}{b_0} \left[\sum_j \Theta_{ij}(L)\beta_{ij} Y_t^*\right] + b_1 Y_{it-1} + b_2 Y_{it-2}$$

$$+ \ldots + b_m Y_{it-m}; \quad i = 1, \ldots, n. \tag{2.17}$$

Examination of (2.17) indicates that the structure (2.7), including feedbacks and interactions in the time demand for factors of production, can be reduced to n separate distributed lag functions, in which *only own past values* of the demand for each factor appear as arguments, without feedback effects apparently present. In addition, the arguments of (2.17) other than Y_{it} are current and lagged values of all variables included in the specification of each Y_{it}^*. Thus, equation (2.17) should be familiar as a general version of the commonly assumed distributed lag structure. All equations in (2.17) could be further reduced to infinite distributed lags of all current and past values of the variables included in Y^*. This amounts to what has been set forth above [see equation (2.10) and related discussion], and there is no need to repeat it.

Evidently, distributed lag models of the form (2.17) characterize most of the literature on time-series input demand. For example, the index of i relating to capital stock in (2.17) yields a formulation that is identical in form to neoclassical investment functions (Jorgenson [1963], Eisner and Nadiri [1968], Bischoff [1971]). Existing short-run employment demand function studies (Brechling [1965], Dhrymes [1969]) can also be considered as special cases of (2.17). Thus, the present model integrates these two apparently unrelated branches of the literature, and alternative estimates of such functions are possible. Note, however, that we have taken into account the *cross* and own adjustments in each equation of (2.17). Thus, a substantially different interpretation of the adjustment process is suggested in our model, compared to what exists in the literature.

As one application of the model, we examine the many distributed lag investment and employment functions that display lag distributions with complex roots and implied oscillatory patterns (Griliches and Wallace [1965], Griliches [1967], and Nadiri [1968]). Such results are questionable on economic grounds, if one considers the source of adjustment lags strictly in terms of own lags with no interrelations present. Under the usual interpretation, it is difficult indeed to account for nonmonotonic convergence to new equilibria on the basis of a single equation model. However, (2.17) shows that the adjustment hypothesis embedded in equations (2.7) has a definable interpretation: Each term of $\{\beta_{ij}\}$ is real; and some inputs show a positive reaction to excess demands of factors by the firm, while others show a negative reaction. However, if $(I - \hat{\beta})$ has complex roots, the distributed lag models of (2.17) must display values of b_i in $\Theta(L)$ that also imply complex roots, generating distributed lag patterns that have cyclical components.

One other implication of (2.17) is worth mentioning. Notice that the own-lag terms in each equation *all* have the *same* set of coefficients b_k. This is a well-known property of the reduced form of a system of difference equations. Previous studies of investment behavior have indicated that adjustment lags for demand for capital are of very long duration (Mayer [1960], Jorgenson [1963]). Such findings have been rationalized in terms of very long gestation periods and large costs of adjustment necessary to change productive capital stock. On the other hand, independent investigations of the demand for employment and hours have also found long adjustment lags (Dhrymes [1969], Nadiri [1968]). A priori, logic suggests that the lags in production worker employment should be substantially shorter than for capital, since adjustment costs to the firm are probably smaller. Thus, the long lags estimated for capital and employment have been something of an empirical puzzle. However, if one accepts the basis of the current model, the puzzle disappears. The terms in (2.17) are identical across equations, so that anything producing

the slope of the trend seems to vary over the span of time studied. Capital stock increased at a rapid rate during 1949–57, but its momentum was checked during the slow-growth phase of the economy (1958I–1960IV) and this sluggishness continued until the end of 1962. Capital stock rose very steeply in the expansionary period 1963I–1967IV. There is some minor retardation of the series at peaks, and it seems to lag behind business cycle turning points by about three to four quarters.

The stock of total inventories (Y_5) fluctuates considerably and has a pronounced trend of 0.465 per cent per quarter. Fluctuations of this variable coincide with the business cycle. During expansions, inventories are drawn down as sales expand, and the reverse often occurs during contractions. But this cyclical behavior, as indicated in Chart 3.5, does not always hold. Part of the reason is that our measure of inventories includes finished, semifinished, and raw materials. The sales-inventory ratio will be affected by how rapidly and by how much the firm replaces its stock of semifinished and raw materials.

The flow variables exhibit interesting behavior. Average hours worked (Y_2) fluctuates around a narrow band of values, displaying a very small trend and at least a two-quarter lead in the early phase of the business cycle. This lead seems to have increased in the latter part of the period. Hours worked are a well-known leading indicator of business cycle activity (Bry [1959], Hultgren [1965]); our measure reflects that fact. The generalized utilization rate (Y_4) fluctuates greatly, but with no real trend (0.0015 per cent per quarter). It leads by one to two quarters at business cycle turns, though its fluctuations have been very small during the long expansionary phase of the economy in the 1961–67 period.

The deflated sales variable fluctuates considerably around a rising trend of 0.81 per cent per quarter and lags behind at peaks and troughs of the business cycle by one to two quarters. The wage variable, w, is largely trend-dominated with little fluctuation; it leads at troughs and coincides at peaks of the cycle. The rental price of capital, c, on the other hand, has an upward trend and fluctuates considerably, mainly reflecting movements in the interest rate. Generally, it leads by about one quarter at turning points of the cycle. The relative price variable, w/c, the ratio of wages to the rental price of capital, has a downward trend of about -0.06 per cent per quarter and fluctuates considerably, rising in the troughs and falling during the expansionary phases of the economy. This phenomenon is due both to downward rigidity of money wage rates in the postwar period and greater flexibility of capital costs over the cycle, at least since 1953.

It is obvious that the input variables mentioned often move in the same direction and tend to reinforce each other. At other times, some variables move counter to others in order to meet output or sales requirements. The lead and lag relations among the inputs suggest the desirability of explicitly taking into account joint responses of inputs to changes in sales, prices, and other exogenous variables in a unified theoretical and empirical framework. Model (2.7), as specified in Chapter 2 and estimated below, is our attempt in this direction and stands in sharp contrast to the usual practice of analyzing the behavior of each input independently of the others.

CHART 3.1

STOCK OF PRODUCTION WORKERS (Y_1), 1947I–1970II

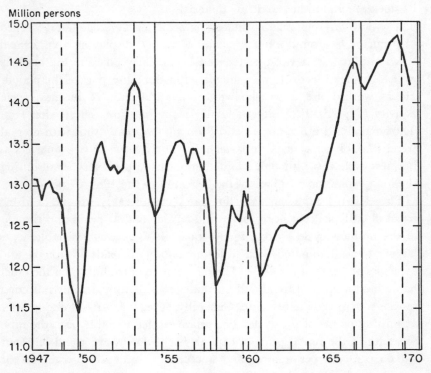

SOURCE: U.S. Department of Labor [1965] and U.S. Department of Commerce, *Survey of Current Business.*

CHART 3.2

HOURS OF WORK PER WEEK OF PRODUCTION WORKERS (Y_2),
1947I–1970II

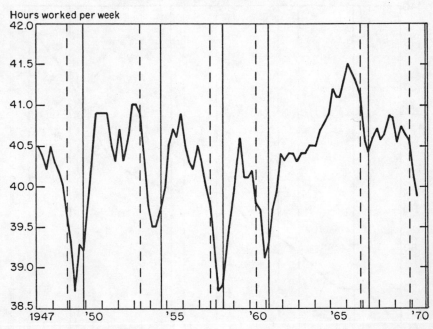

SOURCE: Same as Chart 3.1.

CHART 3.3

DEFLATED CAPITAL STOCK (Y_3), 1947I–1970II

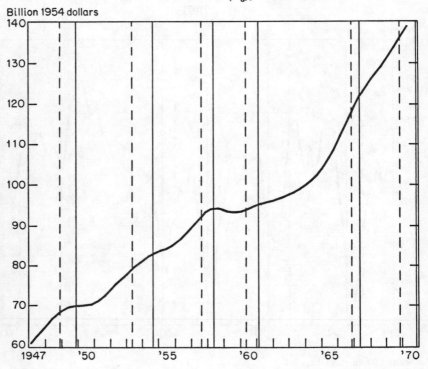

SOURCE: Based on *Survey of Current Business*; for details, see section A, above.

CHART 3.4

UTILIZATION RATE (Y_4), 1947I–1970II

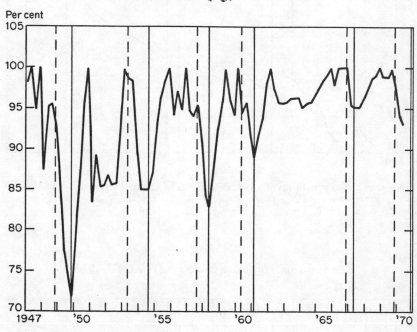

SOURCE: See section A, above.

CHART 3.5

Manufacturers' Total Inventories in Constant Dollars (Y_5),
1947I–1970II

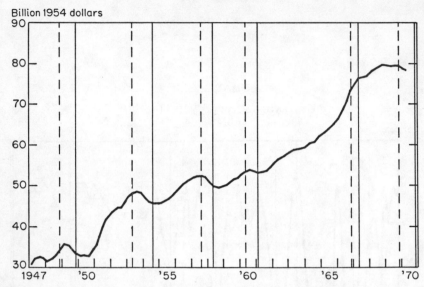

Source: U.S. Department of Commerce, *Survey of Current Business* and *Manufacturers' Shipments, Inventories, and New Orders, 1961–68*; deflated by NBER, using wholesale price data reported in *SCB*.

CHART 3.6

Stock of Nonproduction Workers (Y_6), 1947I–1970II

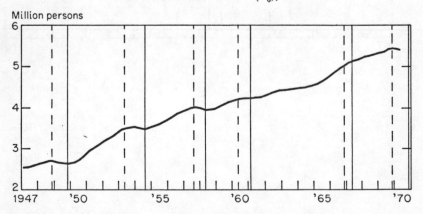

Source: Same as Chart 3.1.

CHART 3.7
DEFLATED SHIPMENTS (S), 1947I–1970II

Billion 1954 dollars

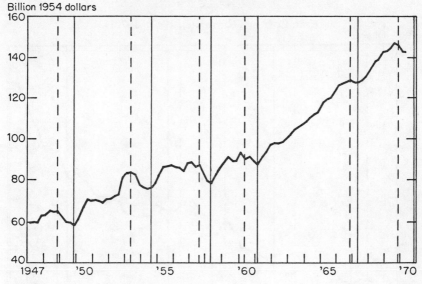

SOURCE: Same as Chart 3.5.

CHART 3.8

HOURLY EARNINGS PER WEEK OF PRODUCTION WORKERS (w), 1947I–1970II

Dollars per hour

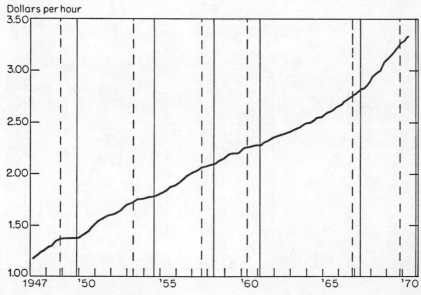

SOURCE: Same as Chart 3.1.

CHART 3.9

User Cost of Capital (*c*), 19471–1970II

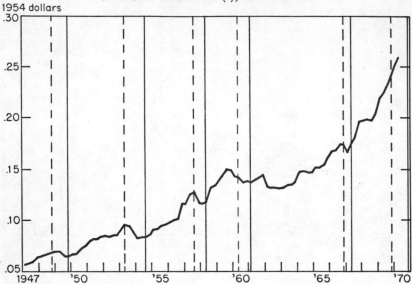

Source: See section A, above.

CHART 3.10

Relative Prices (*w/c*), 1947I–1970II

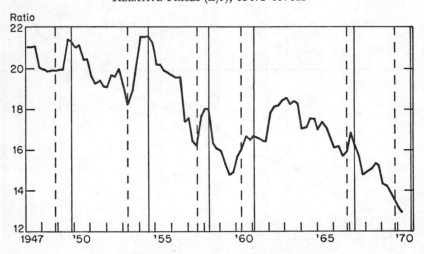

Source: See section A, above.

CHART 3.11

MANUFACTURERS' NEW ORDERS IN CONSTANT DOLLARS (N), 1947I–1970II

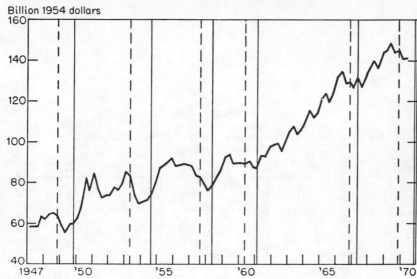

SOURCE: Same as Chart 3.5.

CHART 3.12

MANUFACTURERS' UNFILLED ORDERS IN CONSTANT DOLLARS (ou), 1947I–1970II

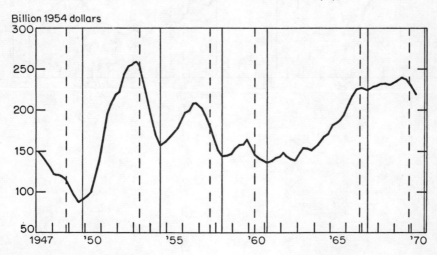

SOURCE: Same as Chart 3.5.

CHART 3.13

RATIO OF MANUFACTURERS' UNFILLED ORDERS TO SHIPMENTS (ou/S),
1947I–1970II

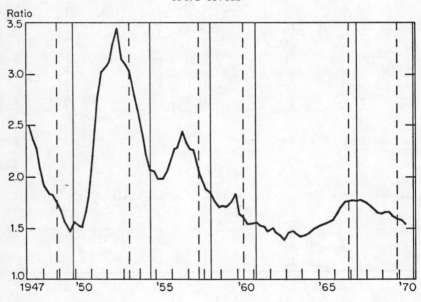

4

ESTIMATION OF THE MODEL: TOTAL MANUFACTURING

THIS chapter contains estimates of model (2.7) using total manufacturing data as described in Chapter 3. An important problem of specification of this model concerns the content of the permanent and transitory shocks that drive the system, as was noted in Chapter 2. Many alternative approximations are possible, and we have experimented with a number of them. These experiments will be summarized in the following chapter. As will be shown there, the main conclusion to be drawn from these experiments is that alternative specifications of sales forecasts do not change the results in any substantive way. Therefore, we present our preferred set of estimates of model (2.7) in which target input values are considered to be log-linear functions of actual sales, relative prices, and trend. This choice is dictated by the ease of computation in view of the insensitivity noted above.

On these assumptions the model is

$$Y_{it} - Y_{it-1} = \sum_{}^{6} \beta_{ij}(Y_{jt}^* - Y_{jt-1}) + \varepsilon_{it}; \ i = 1, 6;$$

and

$$Y_{jt}^* = a_{0j} + a_{ij}S_t + a_{2j}(w/c)_t + a_{3j}T + \varepsilon_{jt}'; \ j = 1, \ldots, 6;$$

where all variables are measured in logarithms and ε and ε' are random variables. The change in each input in period t is taken to be a function of the deviations of all the inputs from their target values at the end of period $t - 1$. In addition, the target value of each input is taken to be a function of sales, relative input prices, and a trend term. T is a trend

55

term taking integer values and with its origin in 1947. Combining these two relations, the equations to be estimated are

$$Y_{it} = m_{i0} + m_{it}S_t + m_{i2}(w/c)_t + m_{i3}T + b_{i1}Y_{1t-1}$$
$$+ b_{i2}Y_{2t-1} + \ldots + b_{i6}Y_{6t-1} + u_{it}; \; i = 1, 2, \ldots, 6; \quad (4.1)$$

where the m_{ij} terms are linear functions of β_{ij} and a_{ij} above, and the b_{ij} terms are naturally related to β_{ij}; that is, $b_{ij} = -\beta_{ij}$ for $i \neq j$ and $b_{ii} = (1 - \beta_{ii})$. The u_{it} are random error terms. As before, all the variables except for trend are measured in natural logarithms.

A. PROBLEMS OF ESTIMATION

Two issues must be considered prior to estimation. One is the question of imposing production function restrictions on the estimates of equations (4.1) a priori. The other is the selection of an appropriate estimation technique.

Although it is computationally inconvenient, imposition of production function constraints is feasible. It requires estimation of all six equations at the same time, with an appropriate adjustment of the over-all covariance matrix. At an early stage of the investigation, we decided not to follow that procedure for three reasons. First, it seems to us that imposing such restrictions makes too much of a presumption that the model is completely correct. If the model is truly "correct" then the unrestricted estimates should satisfy the a-priori restrictions. Second, data limitations already noted necessarily force us to maintain certain hypotheses concerning omitted variables. It might be appropriate to relist these factors. We have no data on "user cost" of labor inputs and hours of work of nonproduction workers. Average wage rates have been used rather than marginal wage rates; inventories consist of goods in process plus final goods rather than each component separately; we have no price data for inventories and nonproduction labor; and our utilization estimates fall short of an ideal measure. Third, the data are highly aggregated. As Fisher [1971] has shown, aggregate data in this context often conceal true underlying microrelationships. Therefore stringent tests of the restrictions undoubtedly require much better and more disaggregated data than two-digit classifications provide.

It is well known that choice of an estimation technique depends on properties of the residuals in the model to be estimated. The presence of serially dependent residuals in almost all economic time-series models is very well documented. Use of ordinary least squares procedures under such circumstances leads to biased results. To avoid this situation, the hypothesis of first-order serially correlated residuals in each equation of model (4.1) is maintained and the implied first-order serial correlation in the residuals for *each* equation is estimated by the Cochrane and Orcutt [1949] search method. This method combines ordinary least squares (OLS) and estimation of the first-order serial correlation of the disturbances. It uses an (internal) ordinary least-squares (OLS) regression to form an initial guess of the first-order correlation coefficient ρ. Then the iterative process finds the value of ρ (denoted by $\hat{\rho}$) which minimizes the sum of squares of the residuals for the particular equation.[1] The range of search for the value for ρ was chosen in the interval -0.9900 to 0.9900. The iterations were terminated either when ρ changed by less than 0.005 from one iteration to another or when twenty iterations had occurred.

We calculated an F statistic, testing the null hypothesis that each equation of the model prior to the ρ transformation did not differ statistically from its counterpart after the transformation. For testing $\rho = 0$ against $\rho = \hat{\rho}$, the approximate F statistic is

$$F(1, n - k - 1) = \frac{[SSR(\rho = 0) - SSR(\rho = \hat{\rho})]/1}{SSR(\rho = \hat{\rho})/n - k - 1},$$

where k is the number of parameters estimated (including ρ), n is the number of observations, and SSR stands for the sum of squared residuals. The calculated values of this test for $n = 80$ and $k = 10$, using SSR from ordinary least squares and generalized least squares for each equation of the model are:

	$\ln Y_1$	$\ln Y_2$	$\ln Y_3$	$\ln Y_4$	$\ln Y_5$	$\ln Y_6$
Calculated F	17.02	3.40	189.3	3.15	53.11	27.43

The critical F values are: 7.04 at 0.01 per cent and 3.99 at 0.05 per cent (1, 69) degrees of freedom. The comparison clearly suggests rejection of the null hypothesis for all equations except for the utilization rates Y_2

1. The procedure uses an internal OLS regression to form an initial guess of ρ, say ρ_0. Then all the variables are transformed by ρ_0 to form the new data set $(Y_t - \rho_0 Y_{t-1})$, and the regression is fitted to the transformed data. The regression coefficients are transformed back into the original variables for re-calculating the serially correlated errors, which provides a new estimate of ρ. The process continues until it converges to a single $\hat{\rho}$.

and Y_4 at the 0.01 level of significance. We accept the presence of first-order serial correlation in each equation.

It should be noted that the Cochrane-Orcutt method applied to our model implicitly assumes serial independence of residuals across equations. If this more complex pattern of serial dependence is present, maximum likelihood methods require estimation of a 6-by-6 matrix of correlation coefficients within and across equations in which the off-diagonal elements are not necessarily zero as has been assumed in our procedure. An investigation of cross-equation serial correlation is presented below.

B. STRUCTURAL ESTIMATES

Structural estimates of model (4.1) for total manufacturing are exhibited in Table 4.1. Judging by the high adjusted R^2 statistics and small standard errors and sums of squared residuals, shown at the bottom of the table, the fit of the model in the sample period is impressive.[2] The goodness of fit is clearly indicated by Charts 4.1 to 4.6, which show actual and predicted values of each variable over the sample period. Note, in particular, that cycle turning points are tracked extremely well, an attribute not often achieved with the same degree of success in alternative models of input demand.

Initial impact effects of sales, trend, and relative prices are indicated in the second, third, and fourth rows of Table 4.1. The sales variable is highly significant in all equations except that of capital stock ($\ln Y_3$) and inventories ($\ln Y_5$). Judging by the magnitude of the regression coefficients, the impact of sales is strongest on the generalized utilization rate ($\ln Y_4$), followed by production worker employment ($\ln Y_1$), and hours per man ($\ln Y_2$). Its effect on nonproduction workers is small, but significant. With the exception of the coefficient in the inventory equation, these results are much as expected. However, inventories serve as a buffer between production and sales and are closely related to decisions of the firm on the acquisition and utilization of the stock of inputs. For example, as inventories of finished goods are drawn down to meet the demands for output, the firm may replenish its stock of goods in process and raw materials; these in turn require higher rates of utilization of the existing stocks of capital and labor and/or additions to them. Therefore, we

---

2. Note that levels of inputs rather than first differences have been used as dependent variables. R^2 statistics would have been lower had first differences been used, though parameter estimates would have been identical to those reported in Table 4.1.

TABLE 4.1

ESTIMATED STRUCTURE OF MODEL (4.1) FOR TOTAL MANUFACTURING

(sample period: 1948I–1967IV; all variables except trend are in natural logarithms)

	Dependent Variables					
Indepen-dent Variables	Prod. Emp. (Y_{1t})	Hours (Y_{2t})	Capital (Y_{3t})	Util. (Y_{4t})	Inven. (Y_{5t})	Nonprod. Emp. (Y_{6t})
Constant	−2.708 (3.266)	.3186 (.8357)	.1137 (.5412)	.8643 (.4129)	−1.344 (1.226)	.0911 (.1529)
Sales	.4394 (12.84)	.1554 (7.891)	−.0048 (.7009)	1.100 (10.62)	.0004 (.0096)	.0531 (2.657)
Trend	−.0004 (6.035)	−.0010 (5.595)	.0001 (.6421)	−.0085 (7.415)	.0012 (1.405)	.0015 (1.889)
Rel. prices (w/c)	−.0177 (.7669)	−.0058 (.7324)	.0017 (.3268)	−.0986 (2.127)	−.0267 (.9263)	−.0112 (.7564)
Y_{1t-1}	.4575 (7.417)	−.0992 (4.040)	.0435 (2.608)	−.2295 (1.658)	.3139 (4.000)	.0352 (.7474)
Y_{2t-1}	.4447 (2.286)	.8525 (8.709)	.0168 (.4322)	−.5874 (1.045)	.5626 (2.115)	.0057 (.2043)
Y_{3t-1}	.1784 (1.877)	−.0137 (.4671)	.9050 (27.94)	−.2794 (1.683)	−.1114 (1.043)	−.0093 (.3150)
Y_{4t-1}	−.0236 (.9932)	−.0820 (5.997)	−.0093 (1.837)	.1953 (2.686)	−.0931 (2.813)	.0408 (2.820)
Y_{5t-1}	.0053 (.1093)	−.0400 (1.982)	.0114 (.9492)	−.6623 (5.892)	.6244 (10.03)	.0153 (.4470)
Y_{6t-1}	−.0649 (.8616)	.0462 (1.814)	.0767 (2.459)	.9811 (6.889)	.3432 (4.047)	.7133 (8.180)
R^2	.9855	.9414	.9999	.9088	.9982	.9995
$\hat{\rho}$	.6665	−.2378	.9330	.0181	.5086	.9255
SEE	.0072	.0047	.0015	.0231	.0099	.0044
SSR	.0036	.0015	.0002	.0367	.0068	.0013

NOTE: Figures in parentheses are t statistics. R^2 is the coefficient of determination; *SEE*, the standard error of estimate; and *SSR*, the sum of squared residuals. For $\hat{\rho}$, see text note 1.

CHART 4.1

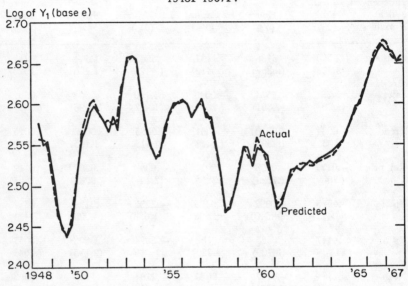

SOURCE: Based on model (4.1.)

CHART 4.2

ACTUAL AND ESTIMATED VALUES OF HOURS OF WORK OF PRODUCTION
WORKERS (Y_2), 1948I–1967IV

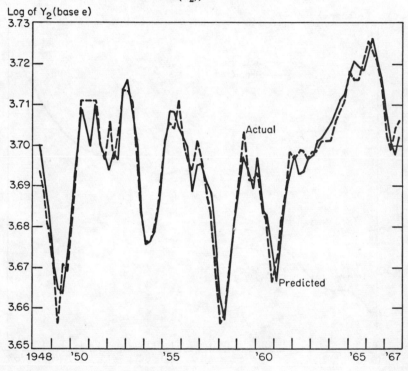

SOURCE: Based on model (4.1).

CHART 4.3

ACTUAL AND ESTIMATED VALUES OF DEFLATED CAPITAL STOCK (Y_3),
1948I–1967IV

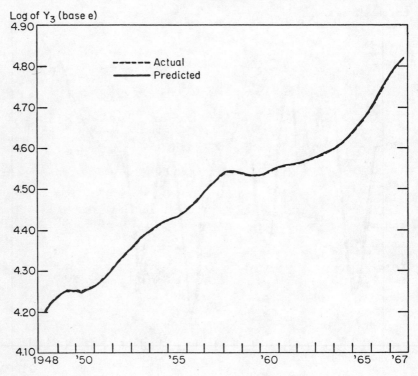

SOURCE: Based on model (4.1).

CHART 4.4

ACTUAL AND ESTIMATED VALUES OF THE UTILIZATION RATE (Y_4),
1948I–1967IV

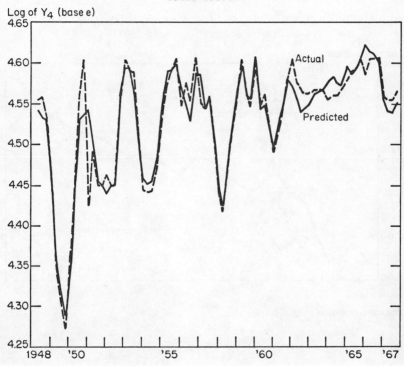

SOURCE: Based on model (4.1).

CHART 4.5

ACTUAL AND ESTIMATED VALUES OF MANUFACTURERS' TOTAL INVENTORIES IN
CONSTANT DOLLARS (Y_5), 1948I–1967IV

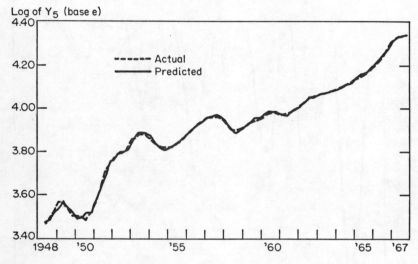

SOURCE: Based on model (4.1).

CHART 4.6

ACTUAL AND ESTIMATED VALUES OF THE STOCK OF NONPRODUCTION WORKERS (Y_6),
1948I–1967IV

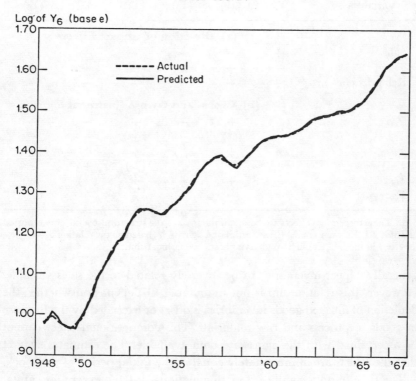

SOURCE: Based on model (4.1).

TABLE 4.2

DIRECTION EFFECT OF EXOGENOUS VARIABLES AND ADJUSTMENT COEFFICIENTS[a]

Independent Variables	Dependent Variables					
	Prod. Emp. (Y_1)	Hours (Y_2)	Capital (Y_3)	Util. (Y_4)	Inven. (Y_5)	Nonprod. Emp. (Y_6)
	(a) Direction of Impact Effects					
Sales	+	+	−	+	+	+
Trend	−	−	+	−	+	+
Rel. prices (w/c)	−	−	+	−	−	−
	(b) Cross- and Own-Adjustment Signs					
Y_{1t-1}	( )	+	−	+	−	−
Y_{2t-1}	−	( )	−	+	−	−
Y_{3t-1}	−	+	( )	+	+	+
Y_{4t-1}	+	+	+	( )	+	−
Y_{5t-1}	−	+	−	+	( )	−
Y_{6t-1}	+	−	−	−	−	( )

a. These directional effects are based on the signs of the structural coefficients reported in Table 4.1. Entries in panel (b) are estimated signs of β_{ij}, based on the relation $\beta_{ij} = -\hat{b}_{ij}$, for $i \neq j$ in model (4.1). The underlying data are in logarithms.

generally expect inventories to be inversely related to the sales variable. However, this relationship is not immutable. It depends on whether the depletion of finished goods inventories is offset or exceeded by the increase in goods in process and raw materials. This compositional effect cannot be ascertained with the aggregate data available. The estimates suggest that the effects are approximately equal in the initial period of the shock.

The time trend is significant in all equations (at 0.05) except for capital stock and inventories. It has negative signs in production worker employment and both utilization rate equations, but is positive in the equation for nonproduction worker employment. The coefficients on the relative price variable are extremely small in magnitude and are insignificant in all equations except in the equation for the general utilization rate, Y_4. This result may be due to high collinearity between trend and relative prices in the sample period, suggesting that the parameters of substitution and technological change cannot be identified in this data. The direction of impact effects is compactly presented in Table 4.2.

The cross- and own-adjustment effects in each equation are shown in Table 4.1 by the columns of regression coefficients of lagged input variables. In each column the own lag coefficient b_{ii}, (e.g., the coefficient of ln Y_{4t-1} in the Y_4 equation) is an estimate of $1 - \beta_{ii}$ in model (4.1). The other coefficients, b_{ij}, are estimates of $- \beta_{ij}$, or the cross-adjustment parameters of the model. Of course, own-adjustment coefficients are expected to be positive and less than unity, and that is the case in all equations. However, cross-adjustment coefficients can take either sign. The direction of these effects are summarized in Table 4.2. Judging from the t values in Table 4.1 and using 1.6 as the cutoff point, 18 out of 30 possible cross-adjustment coefficients are significantly different from zero. Since all cross adjustments need not be nonzero a priori, this is strong evidence in favor of an interrelated model.[3]

The largest number of nonsignificant cross effects occurs in the equation for nonproduction worker employment (Y_6), followed to a lesser extent by production worker employment (Y_1). Even so, both production and nonproduction worker employment strongly interact with all other variables in the system. Moreover, at least one variable interacts significantly with hours of work of production workers and with the generalized utilization rate of nonproduction workers. Therefore, all the input adjustments are interrelated. Furthermore, the signs of the cross adjustments in Table 4.2 indicate that there is no special tendency toward symmetry. In only 9 out of 15 possible paired comparisons (β_{ij} and β_{ji}) are the signs identical.

The signs of the cross-adjustment coefficients, β_{ij}, can be given a worthwhile interpretation in terms of "dynamic substitution." This concept differs in meaning from the conventional concepts of substitution and complementarity, which are equilibrium concepts. In a dynamic setting, firms may temporarily substitute one factor for another, even though the factors are complements in the long run, because short-run adjustment costs make it advantageous to do so. If β_{ij} is positive, excess demand for factor j increases the short-run demand for factor i, and consequently i and j can be considered as dynamic substitutes. If β_{ij} is negative, they can be considered complements.

To illustrate this point, consider the equation for production worker employment (Y_1) in Table 4.1 and also the effect of excess demand for production workers—the coefficient of Y_{1t-1}—in other equations. For all practical purposes, disequilibria in the levels of inventories, non-

3. If 1.85 is used as the cutoff, one-half of the coefficients are significant.

production workers, and generalized utilization rates have negligible effects on demand for production workers in the short run. However, demand for Y_1 is significantly affected by disequilibria in hours (Y_{2t-1}) and in capital stock (Y_{3t-1}). Excess demand for hours and capital stock decreases production worker employment, suggesting short-run complementarity relationships between these inputs. Examining the impact of disequilibrium in nonproduction worker employment on other variables of the system, note a similar complementary relation with capital stock and inventories (i.e., the coefficient of Y_{1t-1} in the Y_{3t} and Y_{5t} equations is positive). However, the coefficients suggest substitution between Y_1 and hours and the generalized utilization rate. Thus, we again note some nonsymmetry in dynamic responses among certain inputs, making it impossible to identify dynamic substitutes and complements in all cases. The feedback relationships among other variables can be interpreted in a similar manner by reference to the signs in panel (b) of Table 4.2.

C. THE GOODNESS OF FIT AND FORECASTING PERFORMANCE

We shall examine the goodness of fit of the model and its performance against an autoregressive model such as

$$Y_{it} = a_{i0} + a_{i1}Y_{it-1} + a_{i2}Y_{it-2} + a_{i3} + Y_{it-3} + \varepsilon_{it}; \; i = 1, \ldots, 6;$$

where ε_{it} is the stochastic residual, and all the variables are measured in natural logarithms. This third-order autoregressive model is essentially a generalization of the familiar naive models often used in the literature (Christ [1956] and Jorgenson-Hunter-Nadiri [1970]). Comparison with an autoregressive model is a very stringent test of quarterly models, and many analytical models often fail to pass it.[4] The sum of squared residuals for each equation of model (4.1) and its autoregressive counterpart were used to compute F statistics. These results indicate that the null hypothesis of no difference between the analytical model (4.1) and the autoregressive model is rejected. Comparison of the turning points predicted by the two models also clearly shows the superiority of model (4.1), especially for the more fluctuating series such as the utilization rate.

Using the structural estimates of model (4.1) reported in Table 4.1,

---

4. More complicated autoregressive models with fourth- and fifth-order lags were used, but the results were similar to those of the third-order autoregressive model.

conditional forecasts for each dependent variable for the next ten quarters can be generated. We used the following performance indexes to test forecasts of the model for the period 1968I–1970IV:

Mean forecast error:

$$m_1 = \frac{1}{n} \sum (Y_i - \hat{Y}_i);$$

Absolute mean error:

$$m_2 = \frac{1}{n} \sum |Y_i - \hat{Y}_i|;$$

Mean square error:

$$m_3 = \left[\frac{n}{n-k} \sum (Y_i - \hat{Y}_i)^2 \right]^{1/2}.$$

The summary statistics on the forecast errors of the estimated equations of Table 4.1 are shown in Table 4.3. Several characteristics of the results

TABLE 4.3

FORECAST PERFORMANCE INDEXES FOR MODEL (4.1)
for TOTAL MANUFACTURING

(forecast period: 1968I-1970II; all variables are measured in natural logarithms[a])

	Prod. Emp. (Y_1)	Hours (Y_2)	Capital (Y_3)	Util. (Y_4)	Inven. (Y_5)	Nonprod. Emp. (Y_6)
Mean error (m_1)	$-.0030$	$-.0003$	.0005	$-.0099$	$-.0027$	$-.0026$
Mean absolute error (m_2)	.0051	.0048	.0007	.0174	.0071	.0038
Mean square error (m_3)	.0059	.0061	.0012	.0219	.0085	.0049

a. The original units are: Y_1, millions of workers; Y_2, hours per man per week; Y_3, billions of 1954 dollars; Y_4, fraction of full capacity; Y_5, billions of 1954 dollars; Y_6, millions of workers.

are worth noting. The mean error, m_1; the absolute mean error, m_2; and the mean square error, m_3, are all very small (as a percentage of the means) for each variable. The mean error of each equation, except for capital stock, is negative, which indicates that, on the whole, the model slightly overforecasts the value of most dependent variables. The m_2's and m_3's are all positive, of course, and naturally larger than m_1 for each equation. The size of forecast errors relative to mean values of the dependent variables in the forecast period are about 0.10 to 0.15 per cent for production worker employment, hours, capital stock, and nonproduction worker employment. It is about 0.065 per cent for inventories and about 40.0 per cent for capital utilization. The latter value results from restricting capital utilization to the interval (0, 1). Our measure uses the logarithms of such numbers, which are often close to zero.

All these summary statistics, though different in magnitude, suggest the same story. They are relatively larger for the capital utilization rate and inventory equations. Forecast errors for production workers exceed those of nonproduction workers and capital stock.

A fruitful way to examine the forecasting performance is to look at the pattern of forecast errors during the period 1968I–1970II and see how closely the level and turning points of the actual data are predicted. The forecast errors are presented in Charts 4.7 and 4.8. Actual and conditional forecasts of the dependent variables are also indicated. The sign and magnitudes of residuals in each equation vary over the period. The model on the whole overpredicts the level of the dependent variables in 1969 and the first two quarters of 1970. The forecast errors are generally negative in this range of the forecast period. The level of the stock variables is very well forecasted for production workers, capital stock, and nonproduction workers. The turning points are perfectly forecast for production workers and capital stock. The model wrongly predicts one turning point and does not predict another one for nonproduction workers in the last two quarters, 1970I and 1970II. In the inventory equation two turning points are missed, as in the hours equation. However, the model is not as successful in calling the turning points of the rates of utilization. As can be seen from Chart 4.7, forecasted hours lag behind the actual series by one quarter. If the predicted values are displaced by one quarter, very few of the turning points will be missed in this series. Once again, this result may occur because actual hours lead all other series used in the model by one or two quarters. The same picture

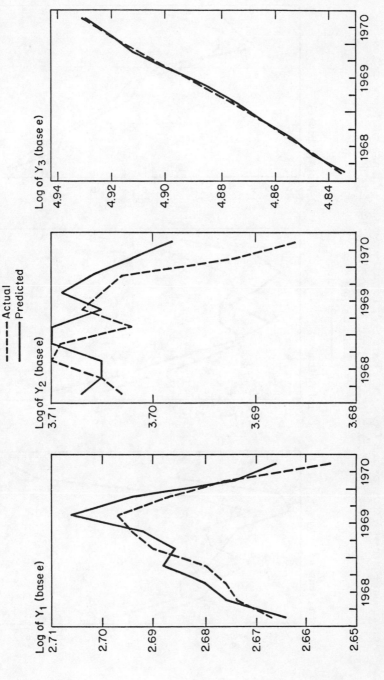

CHART 4.7

ACTUAL AND FORECAST VALUES OF THE STOCK OF PRODUCTION WORKERS (Y_1), WEEKLY HOURS (Y_2), AND CAPITAL (Y_3), FOR TOTAL MANUFACTURING, 1968I–1970II

- - - - Actual
——— Predicted

Log of Y_1 (base e)

2.71
2.70
2.69
2.68
2.67
2.66
2.65

1968   1969   1970

Log of Y_2 (base e)

3.71
3.70
3.69
3.68

1968   1969   1970

Log of Y_3 (base e)

4.94
4.92
4.90
4.88
4.86
4.84

1968   1969   1970

SOURCE: Based on model (4.1).

71

CHART 4.8

ACTUAL AND FORECAST VALUES OF THE UTILIZATION RATE (Y_4), TOTAL INVENTORIES (Y_5), AND THE STOCK OF NON-PRODUCTION WORKERS (Y_6), FOR TOTAL MANUFACTURING, 1968I–1970II

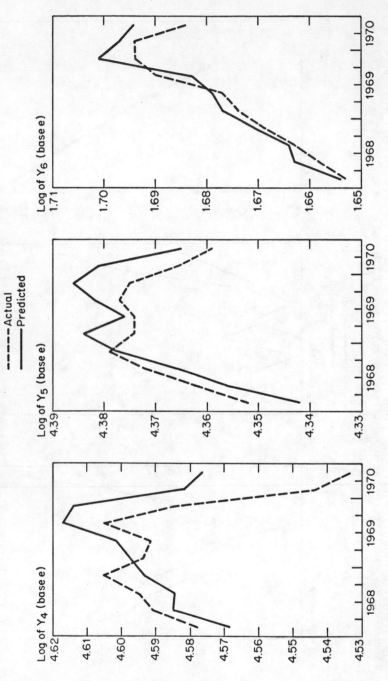

SOURCE: Based on model (4.1).

is drawn for the general rate of utilization. Two out of three turning points are not predicted.[5]

An alternative way of testing forecast performance is based on certain test statistics on forecast errors. These are reported in Table C.1 and indicate no evidence of structural change between sample and forecast periods, confirming the stability of the estimates in Table 4.1.

D. RESPONSE CHARACTERISTICS OF THE MODEL

This section examines distributed lag patterns and estimated long-run scale and price elasticities of demand for various inputs that are implicit in the estimate of model (4.1). As discussed at length in Chapter 2, distributed lag properties of the model are found by transforming the systematic part of (4.1) into an equivalent reduced form. Long-run elasticities are merely the sums of corresponding distributed lag responses in each period.

i. Computational Methods

To summarize the earlier discussion, specifying desired inputs, $\ln Y_t^*$, to be log-linear functions of sales, trend, and relative prices, we have estimated βA_1 and $(I - \beta)$ in

$$Y_t = \beta A_1 q_t + (I - \beta) Y_{t-1}, \tag{4.2}$$

where A_1 is a matrix of fixed coefficients, q is a vector of the exogenous variables: sales, trend, and relative prices (i.e., $Y_t^* = A_1 q_t$), and all are measured in natural logarithms. By recursion, equation (4.2) may be transformed to a reduced form

$$Y_t = \beta A_1 q_t + (I - \beta)\beta A_1 q_{t-1} + (I - \beta)^2 \beta A_1 q_{t-2}$$
$$+ (I - \beta)^3 \beta A_1 q_{t-3} + \ldots. \tag{4.3}$$

---

5. When the forecasting performance of the model for each equation is compared with those of the autoregressive model, above, model (4.1) does better (in terms of the forecast statistics of Table 4.3). This is especially true of inputs such as nonproduction workers and the rate of utilization of capital. The autoregressive model underpredicts *all* the variables during the forecast period, though in the last four quarters (1969III–1970III) the magnitude of this underestimation becomes very small for Y_1 and Y_4. The turning points are more often missed by the autoregressive model in the fluctuating series than in our model. On the other hand, the autoregressive model performs as well in predicting both the level and the turning points of series for capital stock and nonproduction workers.

Equivalently, the reduced form may be expressed in terms of the lag operator L, with $LY_{it} = Y_{it-1}$, and so on. In these terms (4.2) is

$$[I - (I - \beta)L]Y_t = \beta A_1 q_t;$$
$$Y_t = [I - (I - \beta)L]^{-1}\beta A_1 q_t. \tag{4.4}$$

Thus (4.3) and (4.4) are different ways of expressing the same thing. It was demonstrated in Chapter 2 that the matrix $[I-(I-\beta)L]^{-1}$ is a rational function of L, i.e., a ratio of two polynomials in L. The determinant is a sixth-order polynomial in L (fifth order if the restrictions hold), and each cofactor is a fifth-order polynomial. Hence, each term in the inverse is a ratio of a fifth- to sixth-order polynomial. This implies what might be termed "semireduced form" expressions, in which each equation in (4.2) can be written in terms of a *finite* number of lagged values of q and Y's *own* lagged values. Indeed, it is this particular form that is most often utilized in the literature.

At the risk of repetition, an illustration might be in order. Consider a 2×2 case, in which there are only two variables in Y. Then

$$\beta = \begin{bmatrix} \beta_{11} & \beta_{12} \\ \beta_{21} & \beta_{22} \end{bmatrix}.$$

If q has three components, then A_1 is 2×3. Ignoring restrictions, we have

$$[I - (I - \beta)L]^{-1} = \frac{1}{\Theta(L)} \begin{bmatrix} 1 - (1 - \beta_{22})L & \beta_{21}L \\ \beta_{12}L & 1 - (I - \beta_{11})L \end{bmatrix}$$

$$= \frac{1}{\Theta(L)} \{\Theta_{ij}(L)\},$$

with $\Theta(L) = 1 - (2 - \beta_{11} - \beta_{22})L + (1 - \beta_{11})(1 - \beta_{22}) - \beta_{12}\beta_{21}L^2$. Hence, carrying through the multiplication it is seen that

$$Y_{it} = \frac{\Theta_i(L)}{\Theta(L)} q_t, \tag{4.5}$$

where $\Theta_i(L)$ is a row vector of polynomial functions of L related to the $\Theta_{ij}(L)$ terms above (along with the appropriate elements of β and A), and all variables are measured in logarithms, as usual. Multiplying through by $\Theta(L)$ and operating with L, it is seen that $\ln Y_{it}$ can be expressed as a linear function of the natural logarithms of q_t, q_{t-1}, Y_{it-1}, and Y_{it-2}. Therefore, the ratio of $\Theta_i(L)/\Theta(L)$ is the *generating function* of the lag distribution (Griliches [1967]) of the variables in q and $\ln Y_{it}$. In the 6×6 case considered here, $\Theta_i(L)$ is a fifth-order polynomial, and $\Theta(L)$ is sixth order. Thus, expressions such as (4.5) are also equivalent to (4.2) and (4.4).

Define the matrix $B^k = (I - \beta)^k \beta A_1$, which is seen to enter the corresponding lagged value of q_{t-k} in (4.3). In our model there are six variables in Y_t. Hence β and $(I - \beta)$ are square matrices of order six. Moreover, there are three variables in q (ignoring constant terms); thus A has six rows and three columns. Hence B^k has dimension 6×3. Consider the sequence of coefficients in the ith row and jth column of B^k for $k = 1, 2, \ldots$. These coefficients are in fact the (nonnormalized) distributed lag responses of input Y_i to a unit impulse in q_{jt}. Since $(I - \beta)$ and βA_1 have been estimated and reported in Table 4.1, these responses can be calculated by picking off successive ijth elements in B^k. All variables (other than trend) are measured in logarithms; so the sums of these elements are the long-run elasticities of response of each input to the corresponding variable in q. Of course, there is no need to sum these infinite series to obtain long-run responses. Instead, set $Y_t = Y_{t-1} = \overline{Y}$, and let q_t be constant in (4.3). Then long-run responses are computed from $[I - (I - \hat{\beta})]^{-1} \hat{\beta} \hat{A}_1$, which of course yields an estimate of the matrix of "long-run" coefficients.

Figure 4.1 presents responses of distributed lag sales implicit in the estimates of Table 4.1, model (4.1). They have been computed in the manner described above. Similarly, distributed lag patterns can be obtained for relative price responses. Since impact responses of relative prices are so small and unreliable, we do not present them here.

In panel (a) of Figure 4.1, the distributed lag response of production worker employment is related to a unit impulse in sales. Most of the response of employment occurs in the first five or six quarters, and there is no evidence that production worker employment overshoots its ultimate value. The transient sales response of hours per man to sales is shown in panel (b), and that for general utilization in panel (d). These results imply that hours and general utilization are truly variable factors of production and tend to absorb shocks in the face of slowly adjusting stocks. *Both Y_2 and Y_4 overshoot their ultimate long-run values after very large initial responses in the first two quarters so that production and sales are maintained*

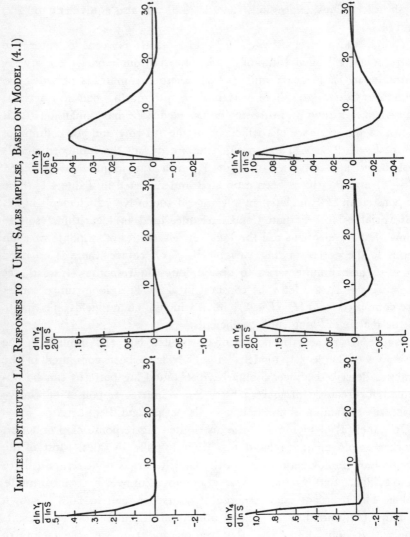

FIGURE 4.1

IMPLIED DISTRIBUTED LAG RESPONSES TO A UNIT SALES IMPULSE, BASED ON MODEL (4.1)

SOURCE: Table 4.1.

76

as other inputs are slowly adjusted. They then slowly converge to their long-run equilibrium values as other inputs steadily increase in response to the stimulus. Panel (c) contains the distributed lag response of capital stock to sales; the curve shows a characteristic bell-shaped pattern found in many other studies. It is noteworthy that these results are based entirely on a first-order *system* and that no second-order lag terms in capital stock have been used. Evidently, the mean lag is long for capital, suggesting that capital stock is the most "fixed" of all inputs.

The distributed lag response of total inventory to sales is shown in panel (f). In interpreting this result, notice that our measure of inventory includes *both* raw materials and goods in process as well as stocks of finished goods. One might anticipate that the latter component would tend to fall after an initial sales impulse and that this would show up in the lag patterns that display some initial negative values. However, the goods-in-process component would not be expected to behave in this manner but, so long as some part of the shock was anticipated, quite the reverse. The net effect of both types of change is shown in the diagram. It is quite clear that the net effect during the first ten to twelve periods after the shock is positive, and so increased holdings of goods in process and raw materials dominate the observations during that period. After about twelve periods, the distributed lag response turns negative, that is, inventories overshoot their ultimate long-run equilibrium value. By that time most of the production labor adjustments have been made, and inventories are run down. Evidently, production is speeded up after the initial shock, and goods in process and raw materials increase sufficiently to meet sales out of finished inventories long after most of the other inputs have been adjusted, and while capital stock is still being built up.

A pattern similar to that of inventories characterizes responses of nonproduction labor. The patterns of initial positive response are like those of production workers, though somewhat delayed and more dispersed over time. This suggests that nonproduction labor is subject to greater adjustment costs than production labor, as might be expected a priori. The pattern in Figure 4.1 indicates some overshooting of the long-run values for nonproduction workers, in distinction to the result for production labor. Perhaps nonproduction workers are more necessary, in the earlier periods, to supervise the great changes in utilization rates that occur at such times. After these changes have damped out, nonproduction labor is laid off. Again, such an explanation is consistent with the notion that labor stocks and utilization as well as capital utilization and inventories bear the brunt of short-run adjustments, while capital stock slowly adjusts to its ultimate long-run value.

ii. Stability

The extended discussion in Chapter 2 showed that the dynamic stability of the difference equation system (4.1) depends on the magnitude of the characteristic roots of $(I - \beta)$. The distributed lag patterns in Figure 4.1 all show that the system is in fact stable. Otherwise, the lag responses would not converge to zero. Another way of examining this behavior is to compute the characteristic roots themselves. For the estimates of Table 4.1 these are 0.9752, 0.8231, 0.8231, 0.5567, 0.5567, 0.0132. The largest root does not exceed unity in absolute value, indicating stability. However, sampling distributions of these statistics are not available, precluding a precise test of stability. The two repeating roots have complex parts that are very small, implying very small oscillations that have no perceptible effect on distributed lag patterns, as is also apparent from Figure 4.1. The convergence properties of the system depend essentially on the largest root, for it dominates response patterns as t grows larger; after the shock, the smaller roots converge at a much faster pace. The largest root is about 0.975 in absolute value. Hence, though the system does indeed converge, its rate of convergence to steady state values is *very slow*. The diagrams clearly reveal this sluggishness to be due to the unusually long lags in capital stock responses.

It is very important to note that the smallest root is very small by comparison with the others. In fact, it is only about 0.013, whereas the next largest is forty times as great, 0.56. As was argued in Chapter 3, production function restrictions depend on the singularity of the adjustment matrix $(I - \beta)$. The magnitude of the smallest root does suggest the near singularity of β, even though no a-priori restrictions were imposed on the estimates. This fact and the overshooting of the distributed lag response for utilization rates are strong verifications of the model specification.

E. LONG-RUN RESPONSE

As noted above, long-run response elasticities are computed from $[I - (I - \beta)]^{-1}\beta A_1 = \hat{A}_1$, since regression estimates in the tables above convey the necessary information about $(I - \beta)$ and βA_1. Computations based on the estimates of Table 4.1 are shown in Table 4.4. These figures have been calculated by using double-precision computer algorithms and should be as accurate as the regression coefficients on which they are based.

Later on, we present evidence of high sensitivity of estimated long-run elasticities to changes in specification. For now, note the following:

i. There is little evidence of significant long-run price or substitution effects in this data. The relative price elasticity for production workers is positive but rather small in absolute value. The relative price elasticity for capital stock is 0.045 and positive as expected. These results are consistent with those of many independent investigations, where estimated time-series elasticities of substitution are found to be very small (Nerlove [1967b]). Relative price elasticities of hours per man are also small, but positive, contrary to hypothesis. The relative price elasticity of nonproduction workers is negative, perhaps because our procedure, in which wage rates and hours per man of nonproduction workers are derived from the rates and hours of production workers, is untenable. The relative price elasticity of inventories ($\ln Y_5$) is positive, suggesting that inventories are substitutes for capital in the "sales production function." The relative price elasticity of the general utilization variable is strongly

TABLE 4.4

LONG-RUN ELASTICITIES FOR TOTAL MANUFACTURING

(all variables except trend are measured in natural logarithms)

Independent Variables	Dependent Variables					
	Prod. Emp. (Y_1)	Hours (Y_2)	Capital (Y_3)	Util. (Y_4)	Inven. (Y_5)	Nonprod. Emp. (Y_6)
Sales (S)	.7301	−.1302	.2933	1.200	.1774	.1595
Relative prices (w/c)	.1067	.1005	.0451	−0.5463	.1634	−.1393
Trend (T)	.0010	.0064	.0051	−0.0366	.0175	.0028

NOTE: Computational formula: $[I - (I - \beta)]^{-1}\beta A$. Each entry gives estimated long-run response elasticity of each input (columns) to a 1 per cent change in each exogenous variable (rows).

SOURCE: Table 4.1.

negative. However, caution is in order in interpreting this result because of the problems, mentioned earlier, of measuring the utilization rate.

Recall that these results are based on very small estimated coefficients on ln (w/c) in the structural equations. Since ln (w/c) has a substantial trend, the impact effects of the structure may only capture transitory price responses and, consequently, our "long-run" estimates of Table 4.3 do not necessarily reflect full responses of permanent changes in relative prices. Also, note again that price variables used in the estimates are far from ideal due to data limitations. Consequently, the estimates may be biased.

ii. There is some evidence of increasing returns to production worker employment, since the sales elasticity is about 0.73, suggesting returns to scale of about 1.3. Note, however, that the sales production function is overidentified, since the restrictions do not hold exactly, and that sales, rather than output, are used. Hence, lack of identification precludes any strong statement about returns to scale. No evidence of long-run scale effects on hours per man is present, consistent with our a-priori hypothesis. This implies that variations in hours per man are almost completely short run and serve a buffer function of insulating changes in demand from changes in input stocks. However, there is some evidence of significant long-run scale effects on general utilization. There is evidence of strong increasing returns to scale for capital stock, inventories, and nonproduction workers, their output elasticities falling far short of unity. Nonuniformity of these effects is not consistent with the type of multiplicative production function postulated in Chapter 2, but might be expected to be the case on the basis of more general considerations. Again, however, the production function is overidentified.

iii. The trend coefficients for production worker employment and general utilization are consistently negative, while the remaining coefficients are positive. Though these results are not consistent with Cobb-Douglas assumptions because embodied and disembodied technical change cannot be identified in that case, they might be consistent with a more general production function.

5

EXPERIMENTATIONS IN SPECIFICATION

THE estimates of Table 4.1 and the computations based on them critically depend on how the model is specified. One issue is to clearly separate lags of adjustment from expectational considerations. The two phenomena (as shown by Nerlove [67] and others) are intertwined and sensitivity of distributed lag estimates may depend on the process of expectation formation. In terms of our model, estimated adjustment coefficients may capture not only genuine adjustment costs but also errors in forecasting exogenous variables. To test the sensitivity of the lag estimates to changes in the specification of exogenous variables, a variety of experiments was performed. The most important are reported in section A below. Only the main conclusions are stated in the text. Specific estimates of the various experiments performed, using total manufacturing data, are to be found in Appendix C, Tables C.2 to C.5. Another issue is that estimated structural coefficients may be affected by strong cross-serial correlation among residuals in various equations. This question is discussed in section B. A third issue, discussed in section C, concerns direct estimation of reduced form equations to check the consistency of model (4.1).

A. SENSITIVITY OF STRUCTURAL ESTIMATES TO SPECIFICATION

i. First, contrast the results of Chapter 4 with those reported earlier by Nadiri and Rosen [1969]. In that work inventories and nonproduction workers were ignored, current real output was used instead of sales, the sample period was shorter (1948I–1962IV), and the statistical methods took no account of serial correlation in the residuals. Nevertheless, distributed lag patterns generated by that model for production workers, hours per man, capital stock, and general utilization are remarkably

FIGURE 5.1

IMPLIED DISTRIBUTED LAG RESPONSES TO A UNIT OUTPUT IMPULSE,
BASED ON 1969 MODEL

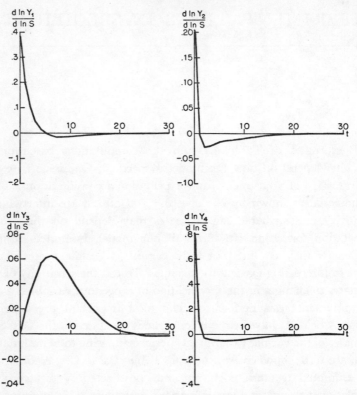

SOURCE: Original model (see Nadiri and Rosen [1969]), omitting total inventory (Y_5) and nonproduction workers (Y_6).

similar to those implied by Table 4.1. These similarities are readily observed in Figure 5.1, which reproduces distributed lag patterns reported in the original work by Nadiri and Rosen [1969]. The overshooting of utilization rates and the approach to equilibrium of stock variables are the same as in model (4.1) of Figure 4.1, in spite of all the differences noted above.

ii. Second, a variety of expectational sales and price variables were generated and used in place of actual variables. We assumed that future values of exogenous variables were generated by a specific stochastic structure. Such a structure was estimated and predicted values from regression estimates were used in the structural equations. In this procedure it is assumed that firms are aware of the stochastic structure generating expected values of sales and relative prices and that the structure remains stable over time. From a statistical point of view, this procedure is equivalent to the use of instrumental variables.

There are numerous ways to forecast exogenous variables, depending on the choice of the stochastic structure and approximations to explanatory variables. For sales, three alternatives have been examined. These are:

$$S_t = a_0 + a_1 S_{t-1} + a_2 S_{t-2} + a_3 S_{t-3} + e_{1t}; \tag{5.1}$$

$$S_t = b_0 + b_1 S_{t-1} + b_2 S_{t-2} + b_3 T + e_{2t}; \tag{5.2}$$

$$S_t = c_0 + c_1 N_t + c_2 N_{t-1} + c_3 \left(\frac{ou}{S}\right)_t N_{t-1} + c_i \Delta P_{t-1} \tag{5.3}$$

$$+ c_5 T + c_6 S_{t-1} + e_{3t};$$

where

S_t = deflated sales in period t (in logarithms);

T = time;

N_t = new orders (in logarithms);

ΔP = changes in the logarithms of wholesale prices;

$\left(\dfrac{ou}{S}\right)$ = unfilled orders divided by sales (logarithms of the ratios).

The first two equations are autoregressive and are often good predictors of quarterly time-series data; equation (5.3) is similar to that developed by Popkin [1965] and Zarnowitz [1962]. Table 5.1 indicates the regression coefficients for these equations and their statistical characteristics. S_t^p and Z_t in the definition of Y_{it}^* in model (2.7) were replaced by predicted values from these equations. Hence, the model to be estimated is similar to (4.1) except that predicted values replace actual values of exogenous variables. A similar procedure was adopted to generate the forecasted values of relative input prices on the basis of an autoregressive formulation such as (5.1) and (5.2). Various combinations of instrumental and actual values of these two variables were tried. Moreover, several values of actual lagged sales and relative prices were incorporated in Y_{it}^* as separate

TABLE 5.1

REGRESSION RESULTS OF AUXILIARY EQUATIONS (5.1), (5.2), AND (5.3) FOR
PREDICTING THE LEVEL OF SALES (S) OF TOTAL MANUFACTURING

(sample period: 1948I–1967IV; all variables except trend
are in natural logarithms)

Indepen-dent Variables[a]	Dependent Variable: S_t		
	Equation (5.1)	Equation (5.2)	Equation (5.3)
Constant	.0365 (.5136)	.7668 (3.281)	.7481 (2.676)
S_{t-1}	1.248 (11.20)	1.145 (10.84)	.6088 (5.911)
S_{t-2}	−.2585 (2.261)	−.3322 (3.141)	—
S_{t-3}	.0038 (.5068)	—	—
N_{t-1}	—	—	.3160 (3.809)
N_{t-2}	—	—	−.411 (1.880)
$\left(\dfrac{ou}{S}\right)N_{t-1}$	—	—	.0273 (1.445)
ΔP_{t-1}	—	—	−.3603 (1.078)
Trend	—	.0017 (3.286)	.0018 (2.597)
R^2	.9818	.9840	.9860
SEE	.0295	.0277	.0269
D.W.	2.00	2.08	1.96

a. Figures in parentheses are t statistics. N denotes new orders; P, product prices; R^2, coefficient of determination; *SEE*, standard error of estimate; *D.W.*, Durbin-Watson statistic.

experiments. The main results of these empirical exercises can be summarized as follows:

a. Using different measures of relative prices did not change the estimates. Most of the information in relative prices is apparently incorporated in the trend and current values of w/c.

b. Results of using different expected sales variables were generally quite similar. To save space, the estimates using predicted values from equation (5.1) are presented in Appendix C, Table C.2. The estimates are quite similar to those in Table 4.1. Again, the distributed lag patterns based on these tables are similar and are shown in Figure 5.2. The similarity to Figure 4.1 requires no further comment.

c. Similar estimates were obtained when several past values of actual sales and relative prices were employed in Y_{it}^*. To save space, those results are not shown. Again, the patterns were similar to those reported immediately above.

d. All the specifications of model (4.1) using unlagged exogenous variables (both instrumental and actual values) were also estimated by ordinary least squares methods, ignoring serial correlation in the residuals. Though the estimates of structural coefficients are obviously biased, these biases did not fundamentally alter the distributed lag patterns shown in the figures. An example is the result in Figure 5.3, which is the model (4.1) specification estimated by ordinary least squares, with no adjustment for serial correlation.

iii. Deficiencies in measurement of the generalized utilization rate were discussed in Chapter 4. The results of Chapter 5 show that this variable plays an important role in short-run adjustments, consistently overshooting its final equilibrium so that output and sales are maintained during the adjustment process. As will be seen below (Chapter 7), this behavior is repeated in disaggregated estimates. To check the sensitivity of responses to possible measurement errors in this variable, the model was re-estimated, and Y_4 was omitted from the system. An alternative rationale for this specification is the assumption that all utilization components in production processes represented by Y_4 are completely variable factors not subject to adjustment costs. Estimates are shown in Table C.3. Corresponding distributed lag patterns are shown in Figure 5.4. Again, the general features noted above apply.

iv. An alternative to using lagged values of exogenous shift variables

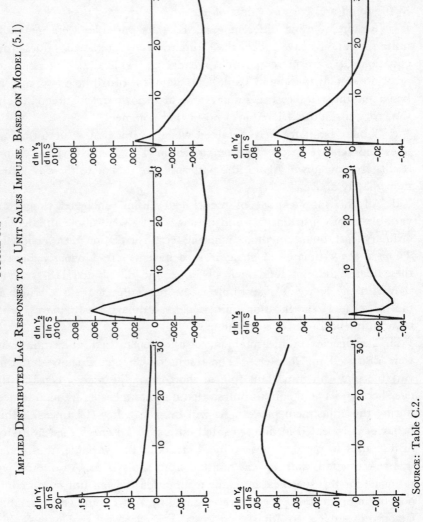

FIGURE 5.2

IMPLIED DISTRIBUTED LAG RESPONSES TO A UNIT SALES IMPULSE, BASED ON MODEL (5.1)

SOURCE: Table C.2.

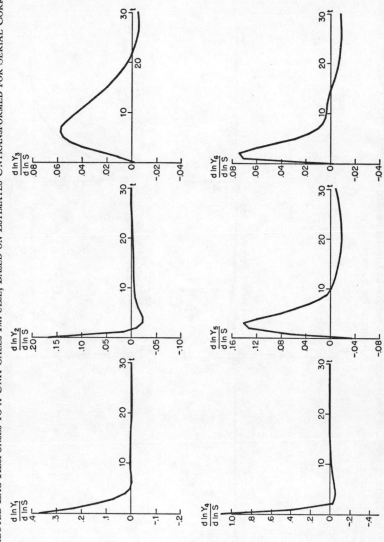

FIGURE 5.3

IMPLIED DISTRIBUTED LAG RESPONSES TO A UNIT SALES IMPULSE, BASED ON ESTIMATES UNTRANSFORMED FOR SERIAL CORRELATION

SOURCE: Model (4.1) estimated by ordinary least squares, and without adjustment for serial correlation.

87

FIGURE 5.4

IMPLIED DISTRIBUTED LAG RESPONSES TO A UNIT SALES IMPULSE, BASED ON MODEL (4.1), OMITTING THE GENERAL UTILIZATION RATE

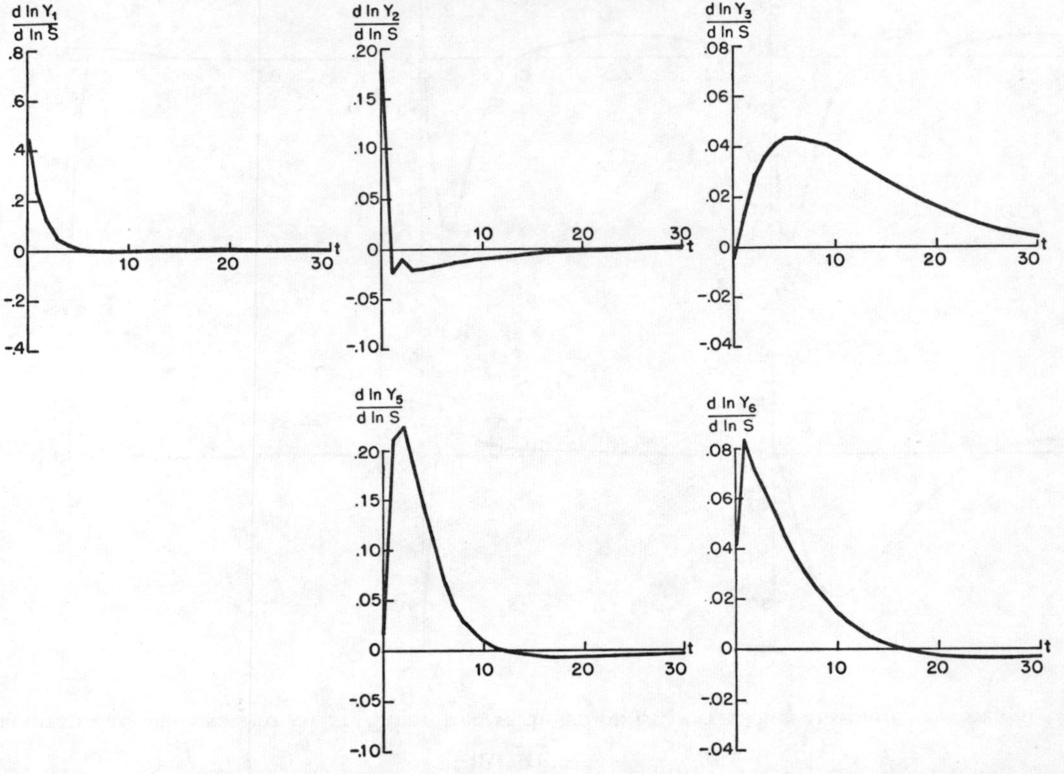

FIGURE 5.5

IMPLIED DISTRIBUTED LAG RESPONSES TO A UNIT SALES IMPULSE, BASED ON ACTUAL CURRENT AND FUTURE SALES

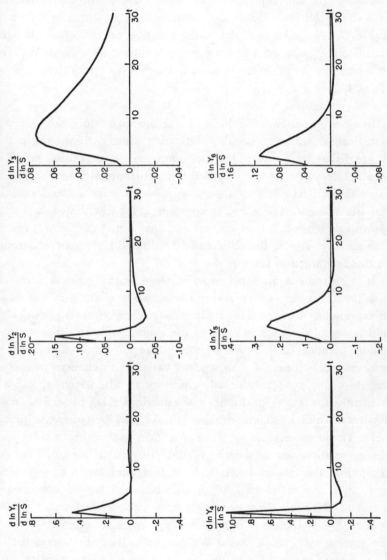

SOURCE: Table C.5.

is to use future values (Mills [1962]) in Y_{it}^*. The theoretical and statistical problems associated with such a procedure will be discussed in the next section. Here, we discuss only the distributed lag responses based on those estimates. In one experiment we included four future actual values of both relative prices and sales. Estimates are presented in Appendix C, Table C.4. In all cases, the future relative price coefficients are not statistically significant. Therefore, we concentrate on a second experiment in which future price terms were deleted. Those results are shown in Table C.5.

In three equations (Y_1, Y_2, and Y_6) the first future sales variable is statistically significant, possibly indicating some current anticipation of future demands. However, the coefficients are, in most cases, rather small in absolute value when compared with current sales coefficients. Most other forward coefficients are statistically insignificant and exhibit instability of signs. Therefore, in computing the distributed lag patterns, shown in Figure 5.5, only current and first future coefficients are taken into account. Again, the patterns of distributed lag responses are similar to those obtained in Chapter 4.

It is clear from all these experiments that the general forms of the distributed lag responses are very insensitive to changes in specifications of exogenous variables. This great variety of experiments provides strong and powerful evidence in favor of the general adjustment structure embedded in model (2.7). However, it should be pointed out that the long-run response elasticities of the dependent variables to changes in exogenous variables displayed substantial sensitivity to alternative specifications. Evidently, the reason for this lies in the distributed lag patterns themselves. Figures 4.1 and 5.1–5.5 often show "thick" tails long after the initial impulse. The long-run elasticity is the area under each distributed lag pattern; hence, small errors in the tail of the distribution are compounded in computing the long-run effects. Note that cumulation of errors occurs long after the initial impulses from which the lagged coefficients are derived and is not in the range of the sample experience. Further, the largest root of $(I - \beta)$ is close to unity, implying slow convergence and therefore the presence of "thick" tails. We conclude, then, that models such as (4.1) are appropriate for estimating short-run and intermediate response patterns and are not well suited for estimating long-run production parameters. We return to this point in a later chapter.

B. ANALYSIS OF RESIDUALS: CROSS CORRELATION

Parameter estimates of the model may be biased because of cross-serial correlation among residuals in various equations. Two issues arise in this connection: (i) concurrent disturbances across equations may be correlated; (ii) nonconcurrent disturbances across equations may also be correlated. The first issue presents no difficulties in the context of our model. There is nothing in principle to suggest that concurrent residuals across equations will be uncorrelated. Indeed, there may be a good reason to think they will be correlated. We have constructed an integrated model in which all input decisions are jointly determined. Hence, any stochastic component arising from the system as a whole, such as in the production function, and so on, would be transmitted to each component symmetrically. This fact provides no difficulties of estimation.

However, cross-serial correlations may exist, that is, $E(\varepsilon_{it}\varepsilon_{jt-1}) \neq 0$ for $i \neq j$, where ε_i is the disturbance in equation i and ε_{jt-1} is the lagged disturbance in equation j. If this is the case, the estimates may be biased. To check this possibility we assemble, in Table 5.2, the simple correlation coefficients of current and lagged estimated residuals from Table 4.1 across equations; $\varepsilon_1, \ldots, \varepsilon_6$ respectively refer to the residuals of the equations $Y_1, \ldots, Y_6$. We note some correlation among the residuals of the equations for production workers and hours worked (about 0.47) and some correlation among the residuals of the capital stock equation and their lagged values. However, in all other cases there is no strong evidence of cross-serial correlations among the residuals of different equations. We also used the multiple correlation to check for cross correlations among the residuals of different equations.

Note that this procedure is biased and at best can be only suggestive. The coefficients are biased because of the presence of lagged residuals across equations. Consider the regressions in Table 5.3. If ε_{it} and ε_{jt} are correlated, then the lagged values of ε_{it-1} are not independent of the error terms in the regression of ε_{it} on ε_{jt-1}. Thus, the coefficients in Table 5.3 may not give the correct results, for the same reason that the Durbin-Watson test is biased when lagged endogenous variables are present in a regression equation. Still, if the true cross correlations are sufficiently strong, they may show up in the regression coefficients. The regressions for ε_3, ε_4, and ε_5 (residuals of the equations for capital stock, utilization rate, and inventories) display no evidence

TABLE 5.2

Matrix of Simple Correlation Among Current and Lagged Residuals[a] of Equation (2.3)

	ε_1	ε_2	ε_3	ε_4	ε_5	ε_6	ε_{1t-1}	ε_{2t-1}	ε_{3t-1}	ε_{4t-1}	ε_{5t-1}	ε_{6t-1}
ε_1	1.0	.496	.368	−.155	−.124	−.070	−.045	−.007	.064	.254	−.069	−.143
ε_2		1.0	.497	−.167	.045	.049	.153	−.061	−.022	−.003	.074	−.1020
ε_3			1.0	−.051	−.038	.004	.112	.040	−.104	.058	.187	−.0111
ε_4				1.0	−.089	−.068	.220	.110	.044	−.079	.016	−.0001
ε_5					1.0	.195	−.037	−.188	−.162	−.040	.091	−.189
ε_6						1.0	.041	.016	−.020	−.335	−.091	.096
ε_{1t-1}							1.0	.489	.374	−.150	−.142	−.111
ε_{t-21}								1.0	.489	−.167	.044	.050
ε_{3t-1}									1.0	−.047	−.057	−.037
ε_{4t-1}										1.0	−.092	−.074
ε_{5t-1}											1.0	.244
ε_{6t-1}												1.0

a. ε_{it} is the residual of the regression equation of $\ln Y_t$ in period t.

TABLE 5.3

REGRESSION RESULTS OF CROSS CORRELATION OF RESIDUALS[a] OF MODEL (4.1)

Independent Variables	ε_{1t}	ε_{2t}	ε_{3t}	ε_{4t}	ε_{5t}	ε_{6t}
Constant	−.00002 (0.069)	−.00004 (0.096)	.00000 (0.005)	.0001 (0.059)	.0004 (0.405)	.0006 (0.082)
ε_{1t-1}	—	.1753 (1.352)	−.0409 (0.944)	−.9224 (1.309)	−.2159 (0.688)	.6018 (3.592)
ε_{2t-1}	.1393 (1.352)	—	.0161 (0.414)	−.2102 (0.331)	.0175 (0.063)	.5431 (3.645)
ε_{3t-1}	−.2939 (0.944)	.1453 (0.414)	—	−1.388 (0.730)	−.3951 (0.469)	−.4201 (0.868)
ε_{4t-1}	−.0248 (1.309)	−.0071 (0.331)	−.0052 (0.730)	—	.0769 (1.511)	.0273 (0.922)
ε_{5t-1}	−.0298 (0.688)	.0030 (0.063)	.0076 (0.469)	.3942 (1.511)	—	.0316 (0.469)
ε_{6t-1}	.2495 (3.592)	.2834 (3.645)	−.0243 (0.868)	.4208 (0.922)	.0948 (0.469)	—
R^2	.2967	.2691	.0492	.0702	.0477	.3794
SEE	.0035	.0040	.0013	.0217	.0096	.0055
D.W.	2.35	2.37	2.02	1.65	1.72	2.35

NOTE: Figures in parentheses are t statistics. R^2 is the coefficient of determination; SEE, the standard error of estimate; D.W., the Durbin-Watson statistic.

a. ε_{it} is the residual of the regression equation of variable ln Y_i in period t.

of cross-serial correlation. There is some suggestion of minor feedbacks in the stochastic structure of the labor subsector, indicating a positive feedback from the stock of nonproduction labor on both hours and employment of production labor. Similarly, hours and employment of production workers have positive and equal effects on the residuals for nonproduction labor. Also, when the own lagged values of residuals were included in the regression equations (not shown) their coefficients were always statistically insignificant.

These effects could be attributed to two causes: (i) the omission of variables such as rental price of labor and hours of nonproduction workers that are expected to affect stock and flow variables in labor decisions symmetrically; and (ii) the tendency of hours to vary in discreet jumps (Charts 3.2 and 4.2), making it likely that any contemporaneous correlations will be pushed backward and that serial cross correlation will result.

It is possible to estimate model (4.1) on our hypothesis of nonzero auto- and cross-serial correlation among residuals by employing full information methods. If the results in Table 5.3 are in fact valid, our model does not capture all feedbacks in the system, and the full information method may be desirable. However, in light of the results in section A, we do not feel that the evidence in Table 5.3 is strong enough to warrant such attempts at this time. This is certainly a proper subject for future investigation. As one step in this direction, we examine the lag structure based on direct estimation of reduced form parameters.

C. REDUCED FORM ESTIMATION

The reduced form system suggests a method for incorporating future values of the exogenous variables and allows us to test whether or not such values should be included.

The model we have discussed so far may be written as

$$Y_t = Aq_t + (I - \beta)Y_{t-1} + U_t, \tag{5.4}$$

where q_t is a vector of expected sales, trend, and relative prices at time t, A and β are matrices of regression coefficients, and U_t is a vector of residuals. A reduced form is obtained by iteration:

$$Y_t = Aq_t + (I - \beta)Aq_{t-1} + (I - \beta)^2Aq_{t-2} + \cdots$$
$$+ U_t + (I - \beta)U_{t-1} + (I - \beta)^2U_{t-2} + \cdots. \tag{5.5}$$

Up to this point, all our efforts have been devoted to estimating A and β in equation (5.4). We now consider estimating these parameters from (5.5).

Estimation of equations (5.5) provides direct information about distributed lag relations and long-run elasticities in the model. For example, the distributed lag of capital stock (Y_3) on sales is given by the appropriate elements in the sequence $\{A, (I - \beta)A, (I - \beta)^2A, \ldots \}$. The long-run coefficients are the sums of these sequences.

Notice that the residuals in (5.5) are weighted sums of current and past disturbances, U_t in (5.4). Thus, direct estimation (5.5) by least squares would not be appropriate. A proper method of estimation would be the generalized least squares technique, requiring a consistent estimate of the (6×6) variance-covariance matrix of the residuals.

Though maximum likelihood techniques would be most appropriate for this problem, we have adopted a second-best procedure for computational convenience. If the covariance matrix is diagonal, generalized least squares amounts to performing separate ρ transformations on each equation of system (5.5). Adopting this method can only be considered a crude approximation of the optimal method of reduced form estimation, for our model requires that $(I - \beta)$ not be diagonal. Consequently, the following results should be interpreted with caution.

The results are reported in Table 5.4, using eight lagged values of sales, plus the time trend and current sales, but ignoring relative prices. Preliminary experimentation indicated that no lagged values of relative price variables were significant. Quite remarkably, the major features of the estimates in Table 5.4 agree very well with their implied values from the estimated structure. The regression coefficients of each variable are very similar to implied distributed lags discussed in Chapter 3. Long-run elasticities computed as the sums of the coefficients on $S_t, \ldots, S_{t-8}$ are indicated in the last line of Table 5.4. By and large they agree reasonably well with those implied by estimation of the structure; and most of the differences are undoubtedly the result of including only eight lags in the table. Once again, this result confirms the insensitivity of the estimates to specification.

In section A, we examined the rationale of including S_t in the structural equations as a forecast of future shocks. The hypothesis that S_t contains most of the relevant information concerning future sales was accepted. The reduced form system (5.5) suggests an additional test, however. Suppose $\hat{S}_{t+1}, \hat{S}_{t+2}, \ldots, \hat{S}_{t+n}$, truly belonged in the structure (5.4), where $\hat{S}_{t+j}$ is anticipated sales j periods hence. If actual sales are a good predictor of anticipated sales, the structural and reduced form equations would include terms in $S_{t+n}, S_{t+n-1}, \ldots, S_{t+1}$ as well as in $S_t, S_{t-1}, \ldots$. As noted earlier, inclusion of forward sales terms in structural equations did not change the basic conclusion that the distributed lag patterns are insensitive to specification of exogenous variables.

A comparable procedure was applied to reduced form estimates. Each dependent variable was regressed on current, four future, and eight past values of sales and relative prices, all adjusted for first-order

TABLE 5.4

LAG DISTRIBUTION FROM TIME DOMAIN REGRESSIONS OF THE DEPENDENT
VARIABLES ON PAST AND CURRENT VALUES OF SALES (S)

(sample period: 1948I–1967IV; all variables except trend are in natural logarithms)

Independent Variables	Dependent Variables					
	Prod. Emp. (Y_1)	Hours (Y_2)	Capital (Y_3)	Util. (Y_4)	Inven. (Y_5)	Nonprod. Emp. (Y_6)
Constant	−.0951 (2.261)	.5767 (13.72)	.0372 (8.049)	−.6308 (1.888)	−.1163 (2.449)	−.0177 (2.457)
S_{t-1}	.2336 (6.980)	−.0052 (.2192)	.0230 (1.230)	.2801 (1.950)	.2946 (4.572)	.1167 (4.334)
S_{t-2}	.0827 (2.493)	−.0156 (.6598)	.0455 (2.447)	−.2359 (1.662)	.1751 (2.737)	.1243 (4.642)
S_{t-3}	.0615 (1.856)	−.0350 (1.485)	.0641 (3.441)	−.1404 (.9972)	.1906 (2.974)	.0908 (3.387)
S_{t-4}	.0339 (.9645)	−.0360 (1.449)	.0617 (3.098)	−.2840 (1.939)	.1996 (2.922)	.0779 (2.717)
S_{t-5}	−.0175 (.5295)	−.0303 (1.284)	.0515 (2.773)	.1239 (.8797)	.2359 (3.688)	.0534 (1.996)
S_{t-6}	.0023 (.0734)	−.0216 (.9397)	.0563 (3.127)	−.1685 (1.219)	.1082 (1.745)	.0317 (1.224)
S_{t-7}	−.0214 (.6759)	.0160 (.7083)	.0608 (3.422)	−.0171 (1.276)	.0148 (.2422)	.0253 (.9880)
S_{t-8}	−.0245 (.7492)	−.0386 (1.677)	.0685 (3.682)	−.0793 (.6208)	.0372 (.5832)	.0234 (.8762)
S_t	.5060 (14.79)	.1678 (7.024)	.0171 (.8770)	.8794 (6.693)	.1870 (2.798)	.1125 (3.997)
Trend	−.0006 (6.723)	−.0002 (.2567)	.0001 (1.769)	−.0004 (.6689)	−.0002 (1.958)	−.0001 (2.669)
R^2	.8895	.6310	.6127	.6917	.6477	.6218
SEE	.0073	.0051	.0042	.0288	.0143	.0060
SSR	.0032	.0015	.0010	.0490	.0121	.0021
$\hat{\rho}$	.9049	.8432	.9854	.6184	.9500	.9840
$\sum_{i=0}^{8} S_{t-i}$	.8576	.656	−.0004	.4486	.1062	1.443

NOTE: Figures in parentheses are t statistics. R^2 is the coefficient of determination adjusted for degrees of freedom; SEE, the standard error of estimate; SSR, the sum of squared residuals. For $\hat{\rho}$, see Chapter 4, note 1.

serial correlation. Again, relative price effects were numerically small and statistically insignificant, a pattern observed throughout the study. To conserve space, only the estimates relating to sales variables are presented in Table 5.5. The coefficients on lagged and unlagged values of S are similar to those in Table 5.4. The forward values are never significant in the capital stock (Y_3), inventory (Y_5), and utilization (Y_4) equations. S_{t+1} enters significantly in all the labor equations but in most cases with numerically small coefficients relative to S_t. Other forward terms (except for S_{t+3} in the hours equation) are insignificant.[1] The same picture emerges when *only* future terms and S_t are included, as shown in Table 5.6.[2]

It is interesting to note that future sales variables display their largest effect in the labor sector, especially in hours per man. This result was also obtained in the test for cross-equation serial correlation in section A. Again, this suggests that there may be some pattern of feedback not captured by model 4.1. However, we emphasize that the future effects are small in magnitude and that the distributed lag patterns based on inclusion of future terms in *either* the structure or the reduced form are little different from those based only on current and past sales.

Furthermore, inclusion of future sales as proxies for future expectations results in biased estimates. At the time that current input and output decisions are made, only past information is available, not future realizations. Even if perfect foresight prevails, so that anticipated sales in period $t + j$ equals the *mean* of realized sales in that period, anticipated sales will be distributed around actual realizations with error. Hence, use of future sales terms introduces measurement errors in both structural

---

1. Table 5.5 contains sums of squared residuals *(SSR)* for computing F statistics to test the null hypothesis that the contribution of the future terms is insignificant. The figures indicate that the null hypothesis can be accepted in every case, except, possibly, that of hours (Y_2).

2. An alternative method is to use a filter such as $1 - \alpha_1 L + \alpha_2 L^2$, where L is the lag operator and α_{i1} and α_{i2} are fixed coefficients estimated from each series of the variables. Define variables

$$S_t^* = S_t - \alpha_{11} S_{t-1} + \alpha_{12} S_{t-2};$$
$$Y_{it}^* = Y_{it} - \alpha_{i1} Y_{it-1} + \alpha_{i2} Y_{it-1}; \quad i = 1, \ldots, 6.$$

Regressing Y_{it}^* on future and past values of S^* provides information similar to that in Tables 5.4–5.6 (Sims [1971]). The regression coefficients and F statistics calculated from these regressions were quite similar to those based on the sums of squared residuals shown in the tables mentioned, and therefore are not reported here. The evidence from these results suggests acceptance of the null hypothesis mentioned above.

TABLE 5.5

LAG DISTRIBUTION FROM TIME DOMAIN REGRESSIONS OF THE DEPENDENT
VARIABLES ON PAST, CURRENT, AND FUTURE VALUES OF SALES (S)

(sample period: 1948I–1967IV; all variables except trend are in natural logarithms)

Independent Variables	Dependent Variables					
	Prod. Emp. (Y_1)	Hours (Y_2)	Capital (Y_3)	Util. (Y_4)	Inven. (Y_5)	Nonprod. Emp. (Y_6)
Constant	−.1331 (2.600)	1.284 (23.99)	.0419 (6.900)	−.4154 (1.113)	−.1112 (1.661)	−.0205 (1.826)
S_{t+1}	.0875 (2.545)	.0866 (3.815)	−.0026 (.1302)	−.0395 (.2435)	.0653 (.9220)	.0555 (1.994)
S_{t+2}	.0227 (.6490)	−.0015 (.0674)	−.0234 (1.129)	.0699 (.4282)	−.0021 (.0301)	.0132 (.4702)
S_{t+3}	.0193 (.5433)	.0628 (2.744)	−.0188 (.8989)	−.1993 (1.219)	−.0798 (1.093)	−.0416 (1.459)
S_{t+4}	−.0492 (1.380)	.0063 (.2998)	−.0124 (.5873)	−.2558 (1.869)	−.0176 (.2387)	−.0464 (1.605)
S_{t-1}	.2350 (6.886)	.0088 (.4047)	.0114 (.5547)	.2422 (1.550)	.2622 (3.695)	.0962 (3.433)
S_{t-2}	.1025 (3.006)	−.0076 (.3457)	.0335 (1.628)	−.2049 (1.304)	.1701 (2.399)	.1305 (4.660)
S_{t-3}	.0971 (2.874)	−.0151 (.6948)	.0614 (3.015)	−.0873 (.5654)	.2176 (3.105)	.1173 (4.242)
S_{t-4}	.0212 (.5984)	−.0429 (1.882)	.0591 (2.750)	−.2928 (1.821)	.2060 (2.789)	.0708 (2.425)
S_{t-5}	−.0132 (.3969)	−.0251 (1.136)	.0491 (2.480)	.1404 (.8874)	.2162 (3.151)	.0447 (1.661)
S_{t-6}	.0098 (.2938)	−.0396 (1.795)	.0532 (2.697)	−.0753 (.4810)	.1166 (1.700)	.0453 (1.689)
S_{t-7}	−.0009 (.0280)	.0244 (1.159)	.0669 (3.459)	.0197 (.1311)	.0465 (.6918)	.0488 (1.854)
S_{t-8}	−.0573 (1.731)	−.0648 (3.238)	.0710 (3.604)	−.0839 (.6489)	.0249 (.3651)	.0038 (.1427)
S_t	.4656 (12.84)	.1447 (6.270)	.0104 (.4718)	.8843 (5.417)	.1585 (2.094)	.0763 (2.545)
Trend	−.0008 (6.764)	−.0004 (3.755)	.0006 (2.013)	.0005 (.7038)	−.0002 (1.558)	−.0001 (2.230)
R^2	.9069	.8380	.6277	.8217	.6708	.6868
SEE	.0070	.0041	.0042	.0268	.0145	.0057
SSR	.0027	.0009	.0009	.0396	.0116	.0018
$\hat{\rho}$	.9011	.5877	.9860	.3528	.9462	.9798
$\sum\limits_{i=0}^{8} S_{t-i}$	.9401	.6144	.1370	.3588	−.1171	1.38

NOTE: Same as NOTE, Table 5.4.

TABLE 5.6

Lag Distribution from Time Domain Regressions of the Dependent
Variables on Current and Future Values of Sales (S)

(sample period: 1948I–1967IV; all variables except trend are in natural
logarithms)

Independent Variables	Prod. Emp. (Y_1)	Hours (Y_2)	Capital (Y_3)	Util. (Y_4)	Inven. (Y_5)	Nonprod. Emp. (Y_6)
Constant	−.0111 (1.915)	.4130 (15.63)	.0565 (20.18)	−1.050 (3.857)	.1870 (7.918)	.0472 (5.819)
S_{t+1}	.0419 (.9571)	.0727 (3.485)	−.0250 (1.129)	.0209 (.1476)	−.0819 (1.059)	.0059 (.1733)
S_{t+2}	−.0603 (1.379)	.0048 (.2307)	−.0260 (1.176)	.1505 (1.046)	−.1120 (1.450)	−.0458 (1.332)
S_{t+3}	−.0759 (1.713)	.0437 (2.075)	−.0079 (.3556)	−.3043 (2.127)	−.2119 (2.710)	−.0733 (2.104)
S_{t+4}	−.0937 (1.972)	.0066 (.3077)	−.0141 (.5870)	−.2747 (2.178)	−.0389 (.4665)	−.0591 (1.587)
S_t	.4966 (10.74)	.1741 (8.269)	−.0347 (1.484)	.8869 (7.129)	.0298 (.3664)	.0595 (1.639)
Trend	.00003 (.5908)	−.0004 (6.470)	.0001 (3.854)	−.0010 (1.756)	.0003 (3.408)	.0001 (3.309)
R^2	.7498	.6676	.2203	.7063	.2607	.3194
SEE	.0107	.0048	.0054	.0288	.0188	.0084
SSR	.0076	.0015	.0019	.0547	.0233	.0046
$\hat{\rho}$	.9883	.8306	.9892	.5019	.9670	.9755
$\sum_{i=4}^{8} S_{t+i}$	.3086	.3019	.1077	.4793	.4149	.1128

NOTE: Same as NOTE, Table 5.4.

and reduced form equations. Current anticipations data are often used in economic models to approximate future events. We used some of these data to construct the expected sales variable, Z_t, in equation (2.7), but the results reported in section A were no different from those obtained by using current sales. It is unlikely that use of other anticipations data would give better results.

It is certainly reasonable to suppose that, when adjustments are costly, firms may "build ahead of demand," by holding input inventories in anticipation of future increases in sales. In the equations for hours and other labor variables, the coefficients of future sales variables may be consistent with this phenomenon. It also implies the possibility of simultaneity between sales and input decisions in the system. At an early stage of the investigation, we decided not to use GNP and similar general aggregate measures as demand shift variables that would serve to avoid the simultaneity issue, because the aggregates are too far removed in time and pattern from the experience of specific industries.

Thus, the results reported in this chapter indicate the potential desirability of using more sophisticated estimation techniques, and taking simultaneity and alternative stochastic structures into account more explicitly. The ultimate problem here lies in the economic theory: The integration of a *dynamic* theory of the firm with that of the market is one of the most important unresolved problems in economics. Nevertheless, the multitude of experiments reported here indicate that dynamic response patterns in our model are extremely robust, given the limitations of theory and data. Alternative estimation techniques that are available (Sims [1971]) are no better than the ones we have employed.

6

DISAGGREGATED RESULTS

AN important test of a model is to estimate it on various bodies of data. Analyzing the behavior of factors of production at the disaggregated level is both interesting and important. Disaggregated estimates throw light on structural changes and possible aggregation biases hidden in the aggregate data. They also provide tests of stability of a model. This chapter contains estimates of model (4.1), using time series data for groupings of Standard Industrial Classification (SIC) two- and three-digit industries, identified by code in the right-hand column of the accompanying table and by name in Appendix A. Our own code numbers, in the left-hand column, are intended for ease of reference, since in many cases, as is evident, our industry groups contain several SIC groups.The data used are quarterly observations, 1954I–1967IV, for individual industries and 1948I–1967IV for total durables and total nondurables. The specification of the variables and sources of the data are the same as those for total manufacturing, discussed in Chapter 3. A summary description of the data underlying estimation of the model for the individual industries is provided in Appendix B. Movements of the variables in the individual industries tend to be similar to those found for total manufacturing, and further discussion is therefore unwarranted.

The chapter is organized in the following way. Industries are grouped into durable and nondurable categories. Structural estimates for all industries are presented in section A. In section B we examine distributed lag responses and implied long-run elasticities of the dependent variables in each industry.

A. STRUCTURAL ESTIMATES

i. Overview

Structural estimates of model (4.1) for all industries are reported in

Tables 6.1–6.17. The goodness-of-fit statistics of the estimated equations, such as R^2, the standard errors of estimate, and the sums of squared residuals are impressive in each case and similar to those noted for the total manufacturing. Goodness of fit and forecasting tests similar to those reported for total manufacturing were also computed for total durables and total nondurables. The results were similar to those for total manufacturing and are therefore not repeated. On the whole, the results conclusively indicate the superiority of the model to alternative specifications based on tests similar to those reported in Chapter 4. Charts of actual and predicted values for each dependent variable in each industry indicate the very good fit of the model during the sample period. They also indicate how well the model tracks turning points of the dependent variables. To save space, only those for total durables (01) and total nondurables (10) are presented here (Charts 6.1–6.12, pages 120 to 131).

There is considerable evidence of serial correlation of residuals in the specification of the model prior to the first-order serial transformation, especially in the stock equations. The values of $\hat{\rho}$ shown indicate generally

Manufacturing Industries Included in Model (4.1)

Nadiri-Rosen Code	Industry Name	SIC Code
01	Total durables	19, 24, 25, 32–39
02	Primary iron and steel	331–332
03	Primary nonferrous metal	333–339
04	Electrical machinery and equipment	36
05	Machinery except electrical	35
06	Motor vehicles and equipment	371
07	Transportation equipment, excluding motor vehicles	372–379
08	Stone, clay, and glass	32
09	Other durables	19, 24, 25, 34, 38, 39
10	Total nondurables	20–23, 26–31
11	Food and beverages	20
12	Textile mill products	22
13	Paper and allied products	22
14	Chemical and allied products	68
15	Petroleum and coal products	29
16	Rubber products	30
17	Other nondurables	21, 23, 27, 31

TABLE 6.1

ESTIMATED STRUCTURE OF MODEL (4.1) FOR TOTAL DURABLES (01)

(sample period: 1948I–1967IV; all variables except trend are in natural logarithms)

Indepen-dent Variables	Dependent Variables					
	Prod. Emp. (Y_{1t})	Hours (Y_{2t})	Capital (Y_{3t})	Util. (Y_{4t})	Inven. (Y_{5t})	Nonprod. Emp. (Y_{6t})
Constant	−2.911 (2.582)	1.165 (2.703)	.2978 (1.285)	2.983 (1.126)	−1.050 (.7102)	−.9400 (1.373)
Sales	.4094 (12.49)	.1271 (9.788)	.0015 (.2667)	1.069 (13.36)	.0829 (2.144)	.0345 (2.069)
Trend	−.0041 (5.337)	−.0001 (.5841)	.0005 (1.453)	−.0067 (3.896)	.00005 (.0398)	.0012 (1.251)
w/c	−.0597 (2.130)	−.0137 (1.341)	.0013 (.1993)	−.2046 (3.265)	−.0085 (.1970)	−.0355 (1.742)
Y_{1t-1}	.5472 (8.236)	−.0628 (2.570)	.0477 (3.076)	−.4448 (2.963)	.2610 (2.751)	−.0436 (.9545)
Y_{2t-1}	.6860 (2.566)	.7016 (6.840)	−.0216 (.4503)	−.7688 (1.219)	.3957 (1.156)	.3090 (2.166)
Y_{3t-1}	.0921 (1.039)	−.0733 (2.241)	.8822 (24.46)	−.3538 (1.761)	−.0240 (.1633)	−.0480 (.4543)
Y_{4t-1}	−.1186 (4.343)	−.0565 (5.568)	−.0059 (1.147)	.3560 (5.711)	−.0508 (1.382)	.0208 (1.347)
Y_{5t-1}	−.1180 (2.415)	−.0394 (2.223)	.0186 (1.408)	−.5077 (4.661)	.5980 (7.989)	.0373 (.9578)
Y_{6t-1}	.1374 (2.693)	.0301 (1.668)	.0444 (1.594)	.6656 (5.999)	.3040 (3.197)	.8126 (9.972)
R^2	.9827	.9589	.9999	.9199	.9972	.8994
$\hat{\rho}$	.1721	.0003	.9059	−.0069	.5925	.9024
SEE	.0118	.0048	.0020	.0300	.0137	.0059
SSR	.0097	.0016	.0002	.0622	.0131	.0024

NOTE: Figures in parentheses are t statistics. w/c denotes relative prices. R^2 is the coefficient of determination; *SEE*, the standard error of estimate; *SSR*, the sum of squared residuals. For $\hat{\rho}$, see Chapter 4, note 1.

TABLE 6.2

Estimated Structure of Model (4.1) for Primary Iron and Steel (02)

(sample period: 1954I–1967IV; all variables except trend are in natural logarithms)

Independent Variables	Dependent Variables					
	Prod. Emp. (Y_{1t})	Hours (Y_{2t})	Capital (Y_{3t})	Util. (Y_{4t})	Inven. (Y_{5t})	Nonprod. Emp. (Y_{6t})
Constant	−1.004	.9121	.1161	−9.209	1.505	−.9527
	(1.827)	(1.790)	(3.638)	(2.855)	(1.443)	(1.507)
Sales	.4237	.0800	.0033	.5172	.0738	.0614
	(23.88)	(8.130)	(1.232)	(8.256)	(3.220)	(6.009)
Trend	−.0047	.0003	.0006	.0013	.0039	−.0004
	(3.265)	(.6838)	(1.778)	(.3966)	(2.720)	(1.088)
w/c	.0074	−.0404	−.0098	−.3495	.0086	−.0489
	(.1103)	(1.338)	(.9497)	(1.808)	(.1112)	(1.919)
Y_{1t-1}	.1615	−.0962	.0252	.1362	.0820	−.0890
	(2.503)	(3.135)	(2.562)	(.6958)	(1.066)	(3.229)
Y_{2t-1}	.4798	.5922	−.1028	2.848	−.3407	.2753
	(1.876)	(4.587)	(2.758)	(3.461)	(1.075)	(2.283)
Y_{3t-1}	.3901	.0353	.8662	−.3056	−.1593	−.0090
	(1.489)	(.3676)	(15.42)	(.4975)	(.6136)	(.1175)
Y_{4t-1}	−.0459	.0074	.0088	−.2377	−.0614	−.0034
	(1.294)	(.3322)	(1.791)	(1.670)	(1.219)	(.1452)
Y_{5t-1}	−.2387	−.0516	.0163	−.0588	.6278	−.0695
	(2.406)	(1.307)	(1.001)	(.2328)	(5.929)	(2.187)
Y_{6t-1}	.3818	−.2136	.0624	−.2153	.2086	1.051
	(2.585)	(3.858)	(2.219)	(.6082)	(1.411)	(22.61)
R^2	.9438	.9175	.9702	.8708	.9533	.9813
$\hat{\rho}$	.5682	.1050	.8479	.1122	.2793	−.2441
SEE	.0208	.0114	.0031	.0729	.0268	.0119
SSR	.0194	.0059	.0004	.2396	.0325	.0064

Note: Figures in parentheses are t statistics. w/c denotes relative prices. R^2 is the coefficient of determination; *SEE*, the standard error of estimate; *SSR*, the sum of squared residuals. For $\hat{\rho}$, see Chapter 4, note 1.

TABLE 6.3

ESTIMATED STRUCTURE OF MODEL (4.1) FOR PRIMARY NONFERROUS METAL (03)

(sample period: 1954I–1967IV; all variables except trend are in natural logarithms)

Independent Variables	Dependent Variables					
	Prod. Emp. (Y_{1t})	Hours (Y_{2t})	Capital (Y_{3t})	Util. (Y_{4t})	Inven. (Y_{5t})	Nonprod. Emp. (Y_{6t})
Constant	−2.000 (2.307)	2.425 (4.429)	.1024 (1.893)	−.1204 (.0362)	.2801 (.2028)	−1.742 (3.412)
Sales	.2929 (7.972)	.1021 (6.029)	.0120 (1.358)	1.175 (10.01)	.1518 (2.021)	.0470 (2.656)
Trend	−.0006 (.6721)	.0010 (2.614)	−.00007 (.1999)	−.0090 (2.992)	−.0009 (.4553)	−.0006 (1.522)
w/c	−.0244 (.4899)	−.0284 (1.352)	.0144 (1.234)	.1416 (.9230)	−.0915 (.8824)	−.0662 (2.880)
Y_{1t-1}	.4625 (4.557)	−.0719 (1.690)	.0469 (1.801)	.1824 (.5899)	−.1188 (.5522)	.2047 (4.418)
Y_{2t-1}	.6449 (2.128)	.3833 (2.953)	−.0297 (.4177)	−.5883 (.6270)	.4127 (.6586)	.3870 (2.748)
Y_{3t-1}	−.0823 (.8340)	.0016 (.0447)	.9106 (21.88)	.7768 (2.749)	−.1536 (.6677)	.0434 (1.031)
Y_{4t-1}	−.0545 (1.598)	−.0124 (.7238)	−.0171 (2.495)	−.0749 (.6538)	−.1150 (1.744)	−.0935 (5.384)
Y_{5t-1}	−.1256 (2.491)	−.1090 (5.421)	.0366 (2.333)	−.4506 (3.017)	.8049 (7.227)	.0094 (.4219)
Y_{6t-1}	.2400 (1.548)	−.0465 (.7375)	.1017 (2.399)	−.0206 (.0442)	.6635 (1.992)	.7536 (10.81)
R^2	.9682	.9586	.9927	.9000	.9607	.9943
$\hat{\rho}$	.1984	−.1759	.7842	.0118	.3781	.0111
SEE	.0130	.0064	.0029	.0428	.0259	.0064
SSR	.0076	.0018	.0003	.0827	.0302	.0018

NOTE: Figures in parentheses are t statistics. w/c denotes relative prices. R^2 is the coefficient of determination; SEE, the standard error of estimate; SSR, the sum of squared residuals. For $\hat{\rho}$, see Chapter 4, note 1.

Disaggregated Results

TABLE 6.4

ESTIMATED STRUCTURE OF MODEL (4.1) FOR ELECTRICAL MACHINERY
AND EQUIPMENT (04)

(sample period: 1954I–1967IV; all variables except trend are in natural
logarithms)

Independent Variables	Dependent Variables					
	Prod. Emp. (Y_{1t})	Hours (Y_{2t})	Capital (Y_{3t})	Util. (Y_{4t})	Inven. (Y_{5t})	Nonprod. Emp. (Y_{6t})
Constant	−3.242 (2.199)	2.145 (4.846)	.0067 (.6648)	−10.28 (1.878)	−1.880 (.3757)	−.9932 (3.002)
Sales	.1495 (1.535)	.1020 (2.637)	.0243 (1.587)	1.096 (4.451)	.2668 (1.089)	−.0456 (.9330)
Trend	.0015 (.8807)	.0008 (1.004)	.0010 (.9272)	−.0154 (4.107)	−.0073 (1.916)	.0012 (.8997)
w/c	−.1356 (2.896)	−.0456 (2.241)	.0058 (.5779)	−.0980 (.9268)	−.2154 (2.010)	−.0533 (1.845)
Y_{1t-1}	.7910 (7.050)	−.0330 (.6740)	−.0260 (.9268)	−.8407 (3.258)	.0199 (.0764)	.0552 (.7630)
Y_{2t-1}	.9794 (2.441)	.1545 (.9411)	−.0253 (.3554)	1.886 (1.946)	.4367 (.4495)	.7451 (3.447)
Y_{3t-1}	−.0791 (.5800)	−.0800 (1.191)	.8568 (13.09)	.1076 (.3803)	.5777 (1.996)	−.0967 (.7919)
Y_{4t-1}	−.0763 (2.100)	.0083 (.5751)	.0058 (.8756)	.4870 (5.338)	.1498 (1.649)	−.0164 (.8627)
Y_{5t-1}	−.0642 (1.490)	−.0445 (2.330)	.0164 (1.580)	−.2760 (2.884)	.7588 (7.811)	.0319 (1.145)
Y_{6t-1}	−.0841 (.8172)	−.0581 (1.297)	.0891 (2.213)	.6410 (2.668)	−.0690 (.2860)	.9427 (13.51)
R^2	.9865	.7092	.9375	.9148	.9632	.9930
$\hat{\rho}$	.0662	.3168	.9635	.4399	.3123	.6118
SEE	.0154	.0060	.0027	.0452	.0427	.0079
SSR	.0106	.0016	.0003	.0923	.0822	.0028

NOTE: Figures in parentheses are t statistics. w/c denotes relative prices. R^2 is the coefficent of determination; SEE, the standard error of estimate; SSR, the sum of squared residuals. For $\hat{\rho}$, see Chapter 4, note 1.

TABLE 6.5

ESTIMATED STRUCTURE OF MODEL (4.1) FOR MACHINERY EXCEPT
ELECTRICAL (05)

(sample period: 1954I–1967IV; all variables except trend are in natural
logarithms)

Independent Variables	Dependent Variables					
	Prod. Emp. (Y_{1t})	Hours (Y_{2t})	Capital (Y_{3t})	Util. (Y_{4t})	Inven. (Y_{5t})	Nonprod Emp. (Y_{6t})
Constant	−3.285	.6354	.0379	1.249	−.9063	−.8101
	(4.980)	(1.538)	(1.108)	(.5523)	(.2892)	(4.033)
Sales	.1916	.0695	.0021	1.213	.1712	.0355
	(4.173)	(2.544)	(2.116)	(7.117)	(1.191)	(1.999)
Trend	−.0043	.0002	.0001	.0003	.0032	.0001
	(2.432)	(.2523)	(.3125)	(.0532)	(.6470)	(.2535)
w/c	−.0346	−.0349	.0084	−.0773	.1963	−.0541
	(.7349)	(1.244)	(.7948)	(.4415)	(1.349)	(2.971)
Y_{1t-1}	.4365	−.0003	.0449	−.0566	−.1562	.0054
	(2.868)	(.0041)	(1.020)	(.0984)	(.3580)	(.8842)
Y_{2t-1}	1.416	.7198	−.0208	−.4991	.2078	.4445
	(4.801)	(4.158)	(.2761)	(.4464)	(.2524)	(3.682)
Y_{3t-1}	.0837	−.0106	.9102	−.8785	−.1371	.0090
	(1.050)	(.2324)	(25.72)	(2.818)	(.6773)	(.2525)
Y_{4t-1}	.0522	.0220	−.0011	−.0470	.1289	.0136
	(1.782)	(1.250)	(.1893)	(.4367)	(1.261)	(1.235)
Y_{5t-1}	−.0425	−.0068	.0078	−.3915	.6913	−.0075
	(1.192)	(.3279)	(.7255)	(2.861)	(7.250)	(.4971)
Y_{6t-1}	.2455	−.1403	.1060	.3749	.2855	.8433
	(1.054)	(1.028)	(1.387)	(.4228)	(.4342)	(8.640)
R^2	.9784	.8788	.9938	.7754	.9888	.9961
$\hat{\rho}$	.3579	.3149	.8654	.4191	.0923	.5214
SEE	.0118	.0070	.0028	.0440	.0416	.0046
SSR	.0063	.0022	.0003	.0871	.0779	.0009

NOTE: Figures in parentheses are t statistics. w/c denotes relative prices. R^2 is the coefficient of determination; *SEE*, the standard error of estimate; *SSR*, the sum of squared residuals. For $\hat{\rho}$, see Chapter 4, note 1.

TABLE 6.6

Estimated Structure of Model (4.1) for Motor Vehicles and
Equipment (06)

(sample period: 1954I–1967IV; all variables except trend are in natural
logarithms)

Independent Variables	Dependent Variables					
	Prod. Emp. (Y_{1t})	Hours (Y_{2t})	Capital (Y_{3t})	Util. (Y_{4t})	Inven. (Y_{5t})	Nonprod. Emp. (Y_{6t})
Constant	−2.175 (1.673)	2.066 (4.196)	−.0255 (.1988)	−.0559 (.2725)	−.2975 (.2787)	−1.992 (5.270)
Sales	.5006 (12.08)	.2110 (9.909)	.0047 (.6438)	1.001 (34.40)	.2014 (4.601)	.0502 (3.683)
Trend	−.0055 (4.963)	−.0016 (2.418)	−.0011 (4.425)	−.0019 (1.343)	.0039 (2.853)	−.0001 (.3773)
w/c	−.1089 (1.398)	.0736 (1.286)	.0050 (.2342)	−.1842 (2.153)	−.1912 (1.692)	.0310 (1.019)
Y_{1t-1}	.3663 (2.850)	−.2456 (3.342)	−.0551 (2.233)	.0258 (.2850)	.1991 (1.323)	.0690 (1.527)
Y_{2t-1}	.3002 (1.454)	.2196 (1.835)	.1318 (3.097)	−.0988 (.5604)	.4011 (1.656)	.2313 (3.230)
Y_{3t-1}	−.0280 (.3428)	−.0254 (.4023)	.8968 (33.76)	−.6435 (3.874)	−.1036 (.8436)	.0753 (2.342)
Y_{4t-1}	−.1023 (1.465)	.0022 (.0523)	−.0247 (1.622)	.0669 (1.118)	−.0949 (1.082)	−.0010 (.0431)
Y_{5t-1}	.0387 (.4482)	−.0186 (.3100)	.0828 (3.672)	−.2408 (2.571)	.4777 (3.987)	.0227 (.6910)
Y_{6t-1}	.1688 (.7999)	.1758 (1.218)	.1825 (3.425)	−.1890 (.8027)	.2665 (.9258)	.6384 (7.987)
R^2	.9708	.8030	.9923	.9663	.9763	.9860
$\hat{\rho}$	−.3822	.1988	.4352	.7752	.1293	−.0980
SEE	.0327	.0166	.0057	.0231	.0341	.0106
SSR	.0482	.0124	.0014	.0241	.0526	.0050

Note: Figures in parentheses are t statistics. w/c denotes relative prices. R^2 is the coefficient of determination; SEE, the standard error of estimate; SSR, the sum of squared residuals. For $\hat{\rho}$, see Chapter 4, note 1.

TABLE 6.7

ESTIMATED STRUCTURE OF MODEL (4.1) FOR TRANSPORTATION EQUIPMENT
EXCLUDING MOTOR VEHICLES (07)

(sample period: 1954I–1967IV; all variables except trend are in natural
logarithms)

Independent Variables	Dependent Variables					
	Prod. Emp. (Y_{1t})	Hours (Y_{2t})	Capital (Y_{3t})	Util. (Y_{4t})	Inven. (Y_{5t})	Nonprod. Emp. (Y_{6t})
Constant	−2.560 (2.842)	.8688 (2.165)	−.0942 (.4819)	−4.529 (1.848)	−4.424 (2.166)	−.8302 (3.585)
Sales	−.0002 (.0041)	.0117 (.5058)	−.0209 (1.154)	1.160 (8.811)	.0556 (.4910)	−.0033 (.0654)
Trend	.0040 (1.822)	.0015 (2.050)	.0019 (2.494)	−.0090 (2.408)	−.0010 (.2962)	−.0001 (.0616)
w/c	−.1027 (2.174)	−.0119 (.7261)	−.0346 (2.274)	.0029 (.0349)	.0145 (.1911)	−.0099 (.2225)
Y_{1t-1}	.9853 (14.61)	.0021 (.0942)	.0336 (1.474)	−.2607 (2.164)	.2564 (2.373)	.1543 (1.871)
Y_{2t-1}	1.135 (3.213)	.7190 (5.861)	.1363 (1.218)	1.074 (1.702)	1.391 (2.445)	1.120 (3.631)
Y_{3t-1}	−.2348 (1.789)	−.0773 (1.752)	.8808 (19.55)	−.1262 (.5631)	.1311 (.6456)	.0781 (.5174)
Y_{4t-1}	−.0872 (2.119)	−.0408 (2.511)	.0076 (.6443)	−.0731 (.7786)	−.1855 (2.315)	.0011 (.0374)
Y_{5t-1}	−.0125 (.1928)	.0026 (.1184)	−.0059 (.2759)	−.2881 (2.480)	.7465 (7.155)	−.0552 (.8644)
Y_{6t-1}	−.0072 (.0926)	.0033 (.1347)	.1004 (3.378)	.4596 (3.691)	.0527 (.4641)	.6234 (5.339)
R^2	.9828	.8852	.9992	.8508	.9689	.8606
ρ	.3509	.1619	.5597	.0008	.0781	.8133
SEE	.0143	.0056	.0041	.0325	.0277	.0115
SSR	.0092	.0014	.0007	.0476	.0346	.0060

NOTE: Figures in parentheses are t statistics. w/c denotes relative prices. R^2 is the coefficient of determination; SEE, the standard error of estimate; SSR, the sum of squared residuals. For ρ, see Chapter 4, note 1.

TABLE 6.8

Estimated Structure of Model (4.1) for Stone, Clay, and Glass Products (08)

(sample period: 1954I–1967IV; all variables except trend are in natural logarithms)

Independent Variables	Dependent Variables					
	Prod. Emp. (Y_{1t})	Hours (Y_{2t})	Capital (Y_{3t})	Util. (Y_{4t})	Inven. (Y_{5t})	Nonprod. Emp. (Y_{6t})
Constant	−1.172	2.782	.3595	−.8903	1.836	−2.898
	(.7341)	(5.666)	(1.642)	(.7529)	(.8071)	(1.288)
Sales	.1546	.0665	−.0022	.8466	.0175	.2157
	(4.414)	(4.161)	(.2149)	(15.48)	(.2744)	(4.555)
Trend	.0010	.0031	.0005	−.0016	.0006	−.0034
	(.8067)	(4.580)	(1.066)	(.6308)	(.2550)	(1.929)
w/c	−.0916	−.0458	.0051	−.0141	−.0510	.0494
	(2.942)	(2.727)	(.4174)	(.2178)	(.8079)	(1.192)
Y_{1t-1}	.5849	−.0576	.1288	−.1884	.2897	.1151
	(8.479)	(1.473)	(4.303)	(1.186)	(2.012)	(1.257)
Y_{2t-1}	.3523	.1212	−.1354	−.0011	−.3875	.0408
	(1.092)	(.7929)	(1.372)	(.0021)	(.6399)	(.0942)
Y_{3t-1}	−.1588	−.2456	.9706	.5052	.2342	.4172
	(1.380)	(3.778)	(18.79)	(1.846)	(.9815)	(2.726)
Y_{4t-1}	−.0248	.0260	−.0014	−.0149	−.1035	.0255
	(.6779)	(1.427)	(.1211)	(.2325)	(1.453)	(.5215)
Y_{5t-1}	−.1548	−.0990	−.0441	−.6988	.5823	.1498
	(2.397)	(3.050)	(1.931)	(5.752)	(4.655)	(1.729)
Y_{6t-1}	.1332	.0493	.0255	−.0805	.2341	.3334
	(1.393)	(1.098)	(.8849)	(.5237)	(1.312)	(2.590)
R^2	.9471	.8901	.9989	.9105	.9905	.9911
$\hat{\rho}$	−.1797	.2280	.4674	.4608	.0992	−.2341
SEE	.0106	.0048	.0032	.0170	.0191	.0146
SSR	.0051	.0010	.0004	.0131	.0164	.0095

Note: Figures in parentheses are t statistics. w/c denotes relative prices. R^2 is the coefficient of determination; SEE, the standard error of estimate; SSR, the sum of squared residuals. For $\hat{\rho}$, see Chapter 4, note 1.

TABLE 6.9

ESTIMATED STRUCTURE OF MODEL (4.1) FOR OTHER DURABLES (09)

(sample period: 1954I–1967IV; all variables except trend are in natural logarithms)

Indepen-dent Variables	Dependent Variables					
	Prod. Emp. (Y_{1t})	Hours (Y_{2t})	Capital (Y_{3t})	Util. (Y_{4t})	Inven. (Y_{5t})	Nonprod. Emp. (Y_{6t})
Constant	−2.401 (2.024)	2.603 (3.288)	−.0674 (.6310)	.9787 (.8754)	−.4500 (.4669)	−.1921 (.5135)
Sales	.3440 (5.077)	.1761 (5.083)	.0079 (.4350)	.9403 (5.696)	.2320 (2.009)	−.0049 (.1151)
Trend	−.0049 (2.519)	.0017 (1.853)	.0003 (.4985)	.0050 (.9014)	−.0066 (1.747)	.0032 (2.308)
w/c	−.0151 (.6626)	−.0143 (1.332)	.0093 (1.075)	−.1189 (1.554)	.0422 (.8337)	−.0701 (3.766)
Y_{1t-1}	.5346 (5.004)	−.0287 (.5533)	.0434 (1.359)	.4201 (1.453)	.2804 (1.402)	−.0304 (.4096)
Y_{2t-1}	.5818 (1.818)	.4480 (2.754)	.0434 (.5151)	−.4531 (.5893)	.3264 (.6039)	.1211 (.6013)
Y_{3t-1}	.2775 (1.925)	−.1978 (2.803)	.9633 (20.10)	−1.130 (2.674)	.4148 (1.465)	−.1200 (1.149)
Y_{4t-1}	−.0072 (.1553)	−.0446 (1.928)	.0081 (.6155)	−.0871 (.7229)	−.0294 (.3502)	.0269 (.8627)
Y_{5t-1}	−.2024 (2.659)	−.0109 (.3052)	.0118 (.4785)	−.4748 (2.127)	.2756 (1.796)	.0663 (1.167)
Y_{6t-1}	.1873 (1.391)	−.1339 (2.053)	.0014 (.0307)	.0669 (.1620)	.6143 (2.230)	.6626 (6.531)
R^2	.9809	.9527	.9982	.7600	.9434	.9956
$\hat{\rho}$	.0019	.3153	.6582	.6071	.5176	.4972
SEE	.0084	.0048	.0022	.0205	.0141	.0052
SSR	.0032	.0010	.0002	.0190	.0090	.0012

NOTE: Figures in parentheses are t statistics. w/c denotes relative prices. R^2 is the coefficient of determination; SEE, the standard error of estimate; SSR, the sum of squared residuals. For $\hat{\rho}$, see Chapter 4, note 1.

TABLE 6.10

Estimated Structure of Model (4.1) for Total Nondurables (10)

(sample period: 1948I–1967IV; all variables except trend are in natural logarithms)

Independent Variables	Dependent Variables					
	Prod. Emp. (Y_{1t})	Hours (Y_{2t})	Capital (Y_{3t})	Util. (Y_{4t})	Inven. (Y_{5t})	Nonprod. Emp. (Y_{6t})
Constant	−2.870 (4.894)	.8273 (1.817)	.2316 (1.145)	−2.599 (1.461)	1.109 (1.135)	−1.352 (5.089)
Sales	.2657 (4.956)	.2126 (4.510)	−.0095 (.6645)	.9106 (4.547)	−.0537 (.5470)	−.0197 (.6437)
Trend	−.0024 (3.699)	−.0016 (3.391)	.0001 (.4823)	−.0092 (4.593)	.0021 (1.971)	.0001 (.5084)
w/c	−.0004 (.0273)	.0115 (.8776)	.00006 (.0106)	.0381 (.7786)	−.0050 (.1756)	−.0060 (.8415)
Y_{1t-1}	.5936 (9.218)	−.0866 (1.925)	.0582 (2.188)	−.2063 (1.230)	.3971 (4.023)	−.0261 (1.056)
Y_{2t-1}	.5008 (3.451)	.6033 (4.873)	−.0288 (.7241)	.3704 (.7330)	.0766 (.2938)	.3679 (4.815)
Y_{3t-1}	.2583 (3.540)	.0316 (.6764)	.9371 (26.65)	−.1982 (1.156)	−.2940 (2.824)	.0359 (1.419)
Y_{4t-1}	.0098 (.4254)	−.0353 (1.602)	−.0035 (.6141)	.1391 (1.389)	−.0755 (1.682)	−.0007 (.0447)
Y_{5t-1}	−.0109 (.2723)	−.0299 (.9989)	.0058 (.4519)	−.4459 (3.807)	.6518 (10.04)	.0088 (.5014)
Y_{6t-1}	−.2268 (2.654)	−.0058 (.0951)	.0645 (1.480)	1.145 (4.635)	.4601 (3.465)	.9385 (24.95)
R^2	.9634	.8618	.9998	.7928	.9964	.9992
$\hat{\rho}$	.5708	.2780	.8878	.0234	.3532	−.0727
SEE	.0062	.0056	.0017	.0255	.0115	.0040
SSR	.0026	.0021	.0002	.0450	.0092	.0011

Note: Figures in parentheses are t statistics. w/c denotes relative prices. R^2 is the coefficient of determination; *SEE*, the standard error of estimate; *SSR*, the sum of squared residuals. For $\hat{\rho}$, see Chapter 4, note 1.

TABLE 6.11

ESTIMATED STRUCTURE OF MODEL (4.1) FOR FOOD AND BEVERAGES (11)

(sample period: 1954I–1967IV; all variables except trend are in natural logarithms)

Indepen- dent Variables	Dependent Variables					
	Prod. Emp. (Y_{1t})	Hours (Y_{2t})	Capital (Y_{3t})	Util. (Y_{4t})	Inven. (Y_{5t})	Nonprod. Emp. (Y_{6t})
Constant	−2.419 (2.957)	.7105 (1.232)	−.0033 (.0637)	−6.739 (2.727)	−1.719 (.4292)	.5968 (2.355)
Sales	.1303 (2.220)	.0402 (1.232)	−.0178 (1.542)	.6121 (4.528)	.8283 (2.080)	.0021 (.0452)
Trend	−.0023 (2.893)	−.0008 (2.056)	.0003 (2.107)	−.0072 (4.109)	−.0024 (.4402)	.0033 (4.743)
w/c	−.0326 (2.169)	.0022 (.2653)	.0058 (1.490)	.1680 (4.773)	.2359 (2.196)	−.0107 (.6714)
Y_{1t-1}	.5338 (5.148)	−.1607 (2.936)	.0308 (1.317)	−.7067 (3.145)	.0884 (.1185)	.2312 (2.373)
Y_{2t-1}	.4407 (2.008)	.7775 (6.372)	−.0038 (.0943)	.8105 (1.607)	.3766 (.2558)	−.2595 (1.490)
Y_{3t-1}	.3349 (2.728)	.1397 (2.147)	1.014 (35.22)	.6747 (2.525)	.1250 (.1428)	−.5815 (4.975)
Y_{4t-1}	.0724 (1.877)	.0174 (.7325)	.0108 (1.513)	.3321 (3.322)	−.4696 (1.923)	.0368 (1.231)
Y_{5t-1}	−.0381 (1.834)	−.0134 (1.161)	.0003 (.0679)	−.2970 (6.192)	.0936 (.6347)	−.0207 (1.080)
Y_{6t-1}	.0646 (.4371)	.0504 (.6473)	−.0010 (.0307)	1.334 (4.180)	1.130 (1.055)	.1001 (.7068)
R^2	.9816	.7568	.9904	.8978	.8276	.9409
$\hat{\rho}$	−.0421	−.3324	.6686	−.3835	.2528	.6194
SEE	.0064	.0040	.0011	.0171	.0399	.0046
SSR	.0018	.0007	.00005	.0132	.0719	.0009

NOTE: Figures in parentheses are t statistics. w/c denotes relative prices. R^2 is the coefficient of determination; *SEE*, the standard error of estimate; *SSR*, the sum of squared residuals. For $\hat{\rho}$, see Chapter 4, note 1.

TABLE 6.12

Estimated Structure of Model (4.1) for Textile Mill Products (12)

(sample period: 1954I–1967IV; all variables except trend are in natural logarithms)

Independent Variables	Dependent Variables					
	Prod. Emp. (Y_{1t})	Hours (Y_{2t})	Capital (Y_{3t})	Util. (Y_{4t})	Inven. (Y_{5t})	Nonprod. Emp. (Y_{6t})
Constant	−.3459	2.739	.0033	.4602	1.972	−2.101
	(1.835)	(4.619)	(.0662)	(.5920)	(1.783)	(2.193)
Sales	.1513	.3087	.0044	.9538	.1177	.0260
	(3.323)	(6.415)	(.1705)	(6.259)	(1.354)	(.3933)
Trend	−.0040	−.0032	.0010	−.0060	.0063	.0023
	(5.705)	(4.395)	(2.194)	(2.542)	(4.867)	(2.405)
w/c	−.0468	−.0249	.0155	.0391	.0979	−.0019
	(2.096)	(1.437)	(1.057)	(.5491)	(3.160)	(.0887)
Y_{1t-1}	.3040	−.1223	.1006	.5270	.5398	.2164
	(2.553)	(1.025)	(1.544)	(1.305)	(2.518)	(1.365)
Y_{2t-1}	.3154	.2889	−.0163	−.1821	−.8709	.1109
	(2.148)	(1.674)	(.2027)	(.3619)	(2.788)	(.4665)
Y_{3t-1}	.2816	−.0920	.9267	−.5546	−.0843	.1477
	(4.167)	(1.549)	(20.96)	(2.489)	(.7914)	(1.886)
Y_{4t-1}	.0434	−.0026	−.0023	−.1561	.0146	−.0522
	(1.282)	(.0664)	(.1250)	(1.352)	(.2049)	(.9585)
Y_{5t-1}	−.1047	−.0174	.0034	−.0819	.6070	−.0047
	(1.463)	(.2906)	(.0820)	(.3465)	(5.652)	(.0617)
Y_{6t-1}	.1309	.2550	−.0167	.3034	−.3190	.4199
	(1.392)	(2.361)	(.3203)	(.9463)	(1.633)	(2.833)
R^2	.9247	.9306	.9697	.6605	.9884	.9807
$\hat{\rho}$	.6743	.1401	.8432	.6076	.1153	.0106
SEE	.0065	.0074	.0038	.0220	.0136	.0106
SSR	.0019	.0025	.0006	.0219	.0083	.0051

Note: Figures in parentheses are t statistics. w/c denotes relative prices. R^2 is the coefficient of determination; SEE, the standard error of estimate; SSR, the sum of squared residuals. For $\hat{\rho}$, see Chapter 4, note 1.

TABLE 6.13

ESTIMATED STRUCTURE OF MODEL (4.1) FOR PAPER AND ALLIED
PRODUCTS (13)

(sample period: 1954I–1967IV; all variables except trend are in natural
logarithms)

Independent Variables	Dependent Variables					
	Prod. Emp. (Y_{1t})	Hours (Y_{2t})	Capital (Y_{3t})	Util. (Y_{4t})	Inven. (Y_{5t})	Nonprod. Emp. (Y_{6t})
Constant	−1.178 (2.545)	2.154 (5.893)	.0460 (2.116)	1.519 (1.625)	.8068 (1.752)	−.1056 (.7881)
Sales	.1320 (5.061)	.1692 (6.452)	.0133 (.6941)	.7166 (5.306)	.1519 (1.715)	−.0404 (.7510)
Trend	−.0012 (1.791)	.0003 (.5210)	−.0005 (.6834)	−.0039 (.9212)	.0042 (1.430)	.0099 (4.920)
w/c	.0001 (.0094)	−.0385 (2.592)	.0195 (1.935)	−.0864 (1.152)	.0832 (1.710)	−.0610 (2.122)
Y_{1t-1}	.6870 (10.36)	−.0979 (1.421)	.1647 (2.827)	.1421 (.3557)	.6708 (2.496)	.6189 (3.762)
Y_{2t-1}	.2060 (1.682)	.1964 (1.632)	−.0612 (.8454)	−.6748 (1.148)	−.9272 (2.474)	−.2500 (1.181)
Y_{3t-1}	.1272 (2.884)	−.0748 (1.662)	.8987 (17.24)	−.3632 (1.378)	.1872 (1.012)	−.1741 (1.325)
Y_{4t-1}	.0410 (1.442)	.0065 (.2316)	−.0227 (1.370)	.0174 (.1265)	.1820 (2.089)	−.0127 (.2622)
Y_{5t-1}	−.0853 (2.884)	−.0359 (1.143)	.0470 (1.694)	−.2999 (1.620)	.3092 (2.473)	−.0650 (.8351)
Y_{6t-1}	.0135 (.2665)	−.0507 (.9542)	.0881 (1.960)	.5205 (1.724)	−.2786 (1.376)	.0154 (.1231)
R^2	.9930	.8261	.9808	.5683	.9534	.9189
$\hat{\rho}$	.0509	.2394	.9295	.6137	.7053	.8505
SEE	.0043	.0040	.0025	.0193	.0124	.0073
SSR	.0008	.0007	.0002	.0168	.0069	.0024

NOTE: Figures in parentheses are t statistics. w/c denotes relative prices. R^2 is the coefficient of determination; *SEE*, the standard error of estimate; *SSR*, the sum of squared residuals. For $\hat{\rho}$, see Chapter 4, note 1.

TABLE 6.14

ESTIMATED STRUCTURE OF MODEL (4.1) FOR CHEMICAL AND ALLIED
PRODUCTS (14)

(sample period: 1945I–1967IV; all variables except trend are in natural
logarithms)

Indepen-dent Variables	Dependent Variables					
	Prod. Emp. (Y_{1t})	Hours (Y_{2t})	Capital (Y_{3t})	Util. (Y_{4t})	Inven. (Y_{5t})	Nonprod. Emp. (Y_{6t})
Constant	−2.517 (3.225)	1.784 (3.897)	.0255 (.8365)	−2.222 (2.186)	−.2410 (.1906)	1.147 (1.207)
Sales	.0310 (.7222)	−.0535 (2.367)	−.0187 (.9042)	.6156 (5.104)	−.1493 (1.589)	.0155 (.3548)
Trend	.0006 (.5217)	.0028 (4.433)	.0006 (.8376)	−.0061 (2.180)	.0069 (2.975)	.0007 (.5987)
w/c	−.0344 (1.413)	−.0481 (3.737)	.0107 (1.035)	−.0733 (1.224)	−.1151 (2.275)	−.0340 (1.367)
Y_{1t-1}	.7126 (8.860)	.0149 (.3590)	.0414 (.8568)	.1661 (.7092)	.7827 (4.396)	.2790 (3.517)
Y_{2t-1}	.4136 (1.886)	.4573 (4.051)	.0276 (.2369)	1.326 (2.010)	.5309 (1.055)	−.0918 (.4261)
Y_{3t-1}	.2988 (5.494)	.0273 (1.011)	.8351 (14.34)	.0128 (.0692)	−.0833 (.6162)	−.1309 (2.598)
Y_{4t-1}	.0772 (1.821)	.0086 (.3813)	.0017 (.1035)	−.0318 (.3189)	−.0782 (.8240)	.0134 (.3078)
Y_{5t-1}	.0604 (1.053)	−.0172 (.5994)	−.0007 (.0239)	.0835 (.4647)	.4936 (3.617)	−.1035 (1.929)
Y_{6t-1}	−.3892 (3.724)	−.2270 (4.256)	.1406 (2.103)	−.4476 (1.374)	.0156 (.0651)	1.072 (10.63)
R^2	.9870	.9185	.9619	.7396	.9936	.9987
$\hat{\rho}$	.1382	.0141	.9409	.6386	.3973	.0731
SEE	.0055	.0030	.0025	.0137	.0112	.0060
SSR	.0014	.0004	.0003	.0084	.0057	.0016

NOTE: Figures in parentheses are t statistics. w/c denotes relative prices. R^2 is the coefficient of determination; *SEE*, the standard error of estimate; *SSR*, the sum of squared residuals. For $\hat{\rho}$, see Chapter 4, note 1.

TABLE 6.15

ESTIMATED STRUCTURE OF MODEL (4.1) FOR PETROLEUM AND
COAL PRODUCTS (15)

(sample period: 1954I–1967IV; all variables except trend are in natural
logarithms)

Indepen-dent Variables	Dependent Variables					
	Prod. Emp. (Y_{1t})	Hours (Y_{2t})	Capital (Y_{3t})	Util. (Y_{4t})	Inven. (Y_{5t})	Nonprod. Emp. (Y_{6t})
Constant	−3.935 (2.210)	3.468 (4.590)	−.2360 (.7966)	−6.389 (1.723)	.7951 (.3766)	−5.120 (2.791)
Sales	.0436 (.5612)	.0471 (1.767)	−.0204 (.5641)	.7242 (5.917)	.0952 (.4920)	.00009 (.0012)
Trend	−.0010 (.9916)	.0009 (2.618)	.0015 (2.840)	−.0053 (3.209)	−.0017 (.6371)	−.0024 (2.286)
w/c	−.0052 (.1608)	.0254 (2.286)	.0045 (.2507)	.1064 (2.086)	−.0115 (.1235)	−.0594 (1.755)
Y_{1t-1}	.9423 (12.63)	.0405 (1.591)	.1769 (4.097)	−.2422 (2.070)	−.1483 (.6997)	−.0476 (.6199)
Y_{2t-1}	1.040 (2.629)	.3114 (2.122)	.2358 (1.734)	.7808 (1.133)	−.8865 (1.152)	.9069 (2.226)
Y_{3t-1}	−.0972 (1.103)	−.0429 (1.446)	.9236 (15.98)	.0957 (.7060)	.5726 (2.113)	.1411 (1.555)
Y_{4t-1}	.0109 (.1830)	.0203 (.9608)	.0055 (.2345)	.2293 (2.339)	−.2129 (1.609)	−.0843 (1.371)
Y_{5t-1}	.0066 (.1232)	−.0192 (1.043)	−.0033 (.1220)	−.1053 (1.240)	.4716 (3.309)	.0366 (.6629)
Y_{6t-1}	.1039 (1.092)	.0196 (.6081)	−.0352 (.6526)	.0248 (.1675)	−.1590 (.5889)	.6663 (6.803)
R^2	.9956	.9529	.9750	.7908	.6875	.9416
$\hat{\rho}$	−.1475	−.3175	.4873	−.3781	.3348	−.1482
SEE	.0119	.0045	.0046	.0215	.0251	.0123
SSR	.0064	.0009	.0009	.0208	.0283	.0068

NOTE: Figures in parentheses are t statistics. w/c denotes relative prices. R^2 is the coefficient of determination; *SEE*, the standard error of estimate; *SSR*, the sum of squared residuals. For $\hat{\rho}$, see Chapter 4, note 1

TABLE 6.16

ESTIMATED STRUCTURE OF MODEL (4.1) FOR RUBBER PRODUCTS (16)

(sample period: 1954I–1967IV; all variables except trend are in natural logarithms)

Independent Variables	Dependent Variables					
	Prod. Emp. (Y_{1t})	Hours (Y_{2t})	Capital (Y_{3t})	Util. (Y_{4t})	Inven. (Y_{5t})	Nonprod. Emp. (Y_{6t})
Constant	−4.291 (2.038)	1.922 (2.531)	−.0071 (.0408)	.0830 (.0615)	1.015 (.8503)	−4.057 (3.626)
Sales	.3240 (4.534)	.2141 (6.465)	.0023 (.2385)	1.074 (11.27)	.0963 (1.387)	.0330 (.8717)
Trend	−.0012 (1.133)	−.0006 (1.094)	−.0005 (2.975)	−.00005 (.0257)	.0035 (2.639)	.0011 (2.042)
w/c	.0374 (1.113)	.0256 (1.399)	−.0009 (.1370)	.0484 (.6871)	−.0771 (1.664)	−.0069 (.3871)
Y_{1t-1}	.6050 (4.794)	−.0390 (.6459)	.0144 (.7858)	.0358 (.2047)	.4509 (3.514)	.1193 (1.781)
Y_{2t-1}	.7639 (2.225)	.4014 (2.391)	.0916 (1.778)	−.5188 (1.060)	−.4736 (1.315)	.4002 (2.196)
Y_{3t-1}	.0433 (.2238)	.0466 (.4970)	.9275 (31.19)	−.2772 (.9345)	−.0100 (.0483)	.2467 (2.401)
Y_{4t-1}	−.1514 (2.261)	−.0262 (.8126)	−.0310 (3.128)	.1221 (1.285)	.0401 (.5788)	−.0621 (1.749)
Y_{5t-1}	−.1266 (1.255)	−.1289 (2.490)	.0444 (2.603)	−.3562 (2.073)	.5692 (4.746)	.0865 (1.616)
Y_{6t-1}	.1642 (.5937)	−.0216 (.1694)	.1006 (2.724)	−.4141 (1.219)	−.3722 (1.448)	.3877 (2.639)
R^2	.9874	.8650	.9995	.8654	.9832	.9971
$\hat{\rho}$	−.3485	−.0026	.2467	.3850	.2609	−.3504
SEE	.0225	.0095	.0027	.0263	.0194	.0119
SSR	.0228	.0041	.0003	.0313	.0169	.0064

NOTE: Figures in parentheses are t statistics. w/c denotes relative prices. R^2 is the coefficient of determination; SEE, the standard error of estimate; SSR, the sum of squared residuals. For $\hat{\rho}$, see Chapter 4, note 1.

TABLE 6.17

ESTIMATED STRUCTURE OF MODEL (4.1) FOR OTHER NONDURABLES (17)

(sample period: 1954I–1967IV; all variables except trend are in natural logarithms)

Indepen-dent Varaibles	Dependent Variables					
	Prod. Emp. (Y_{1t})	Hours (Y_{2t})	Capital (Y_{3t})	Util. (Y_{4t})	Inven. (Y_{5t})	Nonprod. Emp. (Y_{6t})
Constant	−1.684 (4.442)	−.1273 (.2206)	.3086 (1.113)	1.676 (.9664)	3.392 (1.614)	−.8909 (2.738)
Sales	.0794 (2.233)	.0625 (1.548)	.0373 (1.574)	.8112 (6.886)	.1958 (1.128)	.0468 (1.788)
Trend	.0002 (.5197)	.00007 (.1377)	−.00006 (.1729)	−.0046 (2.838)	−.0007 (.2917)	.00003 (.0877)
w/c	−.0346 (2.384)	−.0329 (2.350)	−.0050 (.5405)	−.1030 (2.560)	.0873 (1.313)	−.0197) (2.000)
Y_{1t-}	.6144 (5.413)	−.0756 (.7249)	.1667 (2.340)	1.467 (4.920)	.8206 (1.618)	.0820 (1.094)
Y_{2t-1}	.4900 (3.546)	.8944 (6.905)	−.1665 (1.898)	−1.160 (3.135)	−.9740 (1.555)	.1263 (1.362)
Y_{3t-1}	.2221 (4.906)	.1487 (3.749)	.9907 (35.62)	.0196 (.1731)	−.2161 (1.099)	.0727 (2.516)
Y_{t-1}	.0174 (.5892)	−.0299 (.8453)	.0125 (.6260)	.2495 (2.408)	−.0502 (.3398)	.0090 (.4021)
Y_{5t-1}	−.0343 (.9353)	.0195 (.5034)	.0245 (1.015)	−.1775 (1.587)	.6322 (3.604)	.0109 (.4160)
Y_{6t-1}	−.3063 (1.947)	−.3427 (2.292)	−.0877 (.8793)	−1.280 (2.991)	.2130 (.2987)	.7555 (7.142)
R^2	.9804	.8002	.9988	.8166	.9433	.9979
$\hat{\rho}$	.1766	−.3125	.0558	−.3781	0.0	−.0440
SEE	.0052	.0063	.0035	.0187	.0257	.0038
SSR	.0012	.0017	.0005	.0158	.0297	.0006

NOTE: Figures in parentheses are t statistics. w/c denotes relative prices. R^2 is the coefficient of determination; *SEE*, the standard error of estimate; *SSR*, the sum of squared residuals. For $\hat{\rho}$, see Chapter 4, note 1.

CHART 6.1

ACTUAL AND ESTIMATED VALUES OF THE STOCK OF PRODUCTION WORKERS (Y_1),
TOTAL DURABLES, 1948I–1967IV

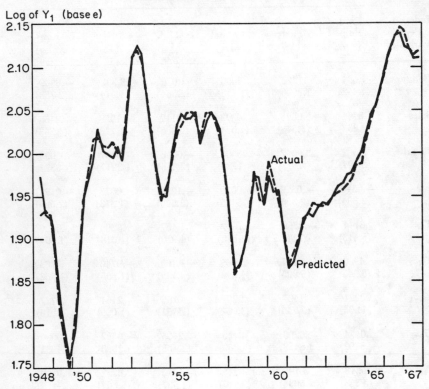

Log of Y_1 (base e)

SOURCE: Based on model (4.1).

CHART 6.2

ACTUAL AND ESTIMATED VALUES OF HOURS OF WORK OF PRODUCTION
WORKERS (Y_2), TOTAL DURABLES, 1948I–1967IV

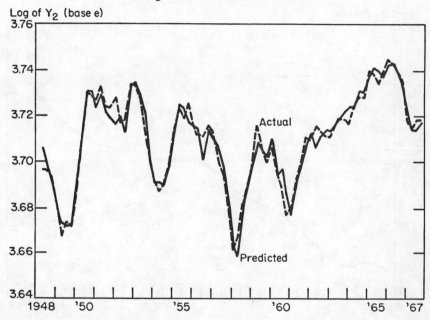

Log of Y_2 (base e)

SOURCE: Based on model (4.1).

CHART 6.3

Actual and Estimated Values of Capital Stock (Y_3), Total Durables, 1948I–1967IV

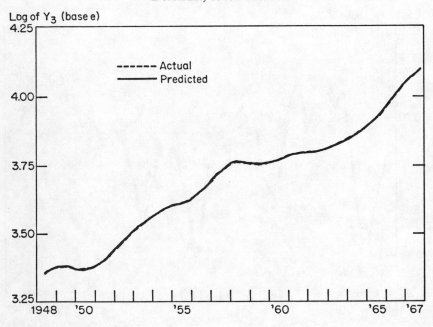

Source: Based on model (4.1).

CHART 6.4

ACTUAL AND ESTIMATED VALUES OF THE UTILIZATION RATE (Y_4),
TOTAL DURABLES, 1948I–1967IV

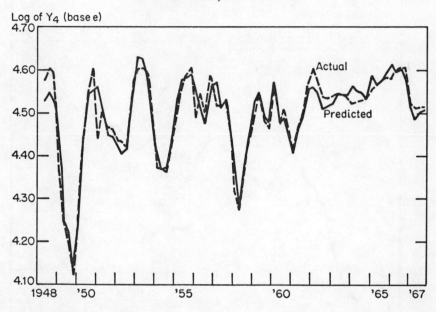

SOURCE: Based on model (4.1).

CHART 6.5

ACTUAL AND ESTIMATED VALUES OF TOTAL INVENTORIES (Y_5),
TOTAL DURABLES, 1948I–1967IV

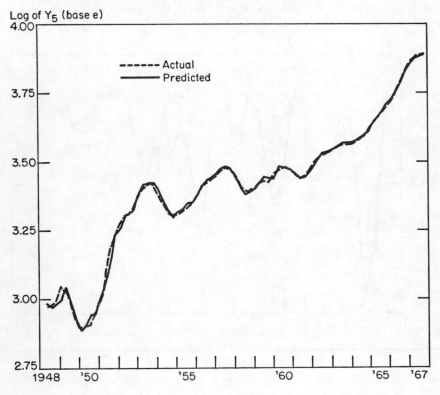

SOURCE: Based on model (4.1).

CHART 6.6

ACTUAL AND ESTIMATED VALUES OF THE STOCK OF NONPRODUCTION WORKERS (Y_6),
TOTAL DURABLES, 1948I–1967IV

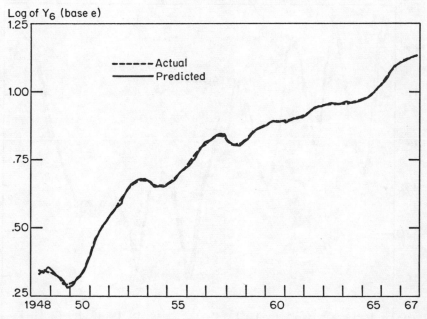

SOURCE: Based on model (4.1).

CHART 6.7

ACTUAL AND ESTIMATED VALUES OF THE STOCK OF PRODUCTION WORKERS (Y_1),
TOTAL NONDURABLES, 1948I–1967IV

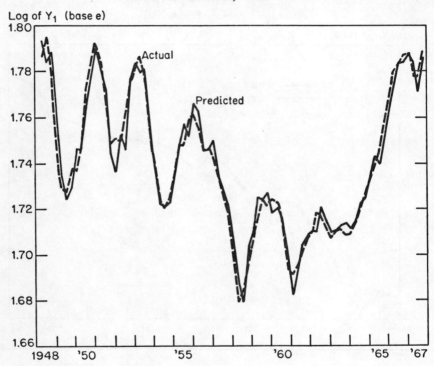

SOURCE: Based on model (4.1).

CHART 6.8

ACTUAL AND ESTIMATED VALUES OF HOURS OF WORK OF PRODUCTION WORKERS (Y_2),
TOTAL NONDURABLES, 1948I–1967IV

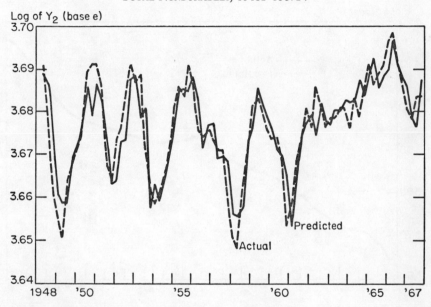

SOURCE: Based on model (4.1).

CHART 6.9

<small>ACTUAL AND ESTIMATED VALUES OF CAPITAL STOCK (Y_3), TOTAL NONDURABLES,</small>
1948I–1967IV

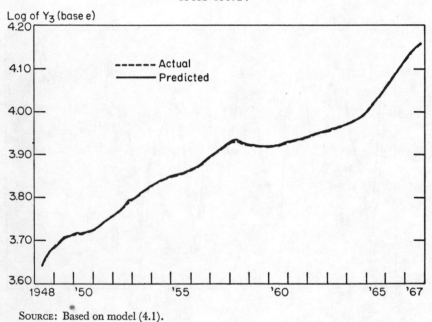

SOURCE: Based on model (4.1).

CHART 6.10

ACTUAL AND ESTIMATED VALUES OF THE UTILIZATION RATE (Y_4), TOTAL
NONDURABLES, 1948I–1967IV

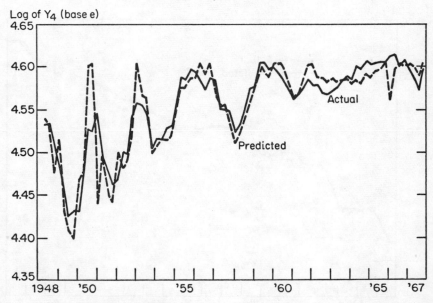

SOURCE: Based on model (4.1).

CHART 6.11

ACTUAL AND ESTIMATED VALUES OF TOTAL INVENTORIES (Y_5),
TOTAL NONDURABLES, 1948I–1967IV

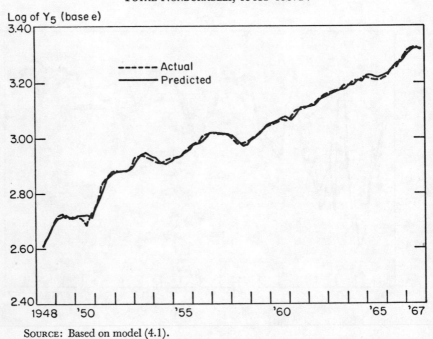

Log of Y_5 (base e)

SOURCE: Based on model (4.1).

CHART 6.12

ACTUAL AND ESTIMATED VALUES OF THE STOCK OF NONPRODUCTION WORKERS (Y_6),
TOTAL NONDURABLES, 1948I–1967IV

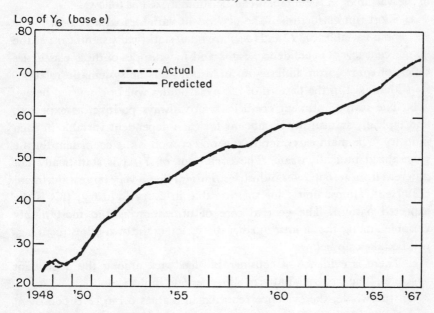

SOURCE: Based on model (4.1).

high serial correlation in the capital stock variable, Y_3. There is no evidence of any systematic pattern among estimated values of ρ for stock equations, though the values are generally higher than those for the flow variables. However, this relation does not always hold, for example, in motor vehicles, other durables, or chemical and allied products. In the nondurable industries, the general rate of utilization, Y_4, shows large values of ρ.

The over-all picture that emerges from consideration of the coefficients of the variables in these tables can be summarized as follows:

a. Short-run elasticities of the dependent variables with respect to the exogenous variables S_t, T, and (w/c) are often statistically significant at the 95 per cent level of confidence. Signs and magnitudes of these elasticities differ, of course, from industry to industry, and the systematic relationships that exist in the pattern of these elasticities will be discussed below.

b. The own-adjustment coefficients are always positive, as expected, and typically statistically significant for each dependent variable in each industry. The main exception to this observation is the coefficient for the generalized utilization rate: The coefficient of Y_{4t-1} is statistically not different from zero in most industries. This implies a very large adjustment coefficient, almost unity, for this variable in every industry; this is the expected pattern. The general rate of utilization is the most highly variable among the inputs. Further discussion of the own-adjustment lags will be taken up below.

c. There is evidence of considerable feedback among the dependent variables. The feedback patterns differ among industries.

On the whole, the evidence reported in Tables 6.1–6.17 is consistent with the a-priori specification of our model. Not only are the underlying data successfully explained, but the adjustment structure postulated by model (4.1) is also borne out by the estimates.

ii. Short-Run Elasticities

Impact elasticities of each dependent variable with respect to the exogenous variables S, (w/c), and T are indicated in the top rows of each table. Specific features and variations from industry to industry can be summarized briefly.

a. *Sales elasticities.* The short-run elasticities of all dependent variables (except capital stock, Y_3) are positive and often statistically significant.

Their magnitudes in the durable industries are generally larger than in the nondurable industries. Capital stock, Y_3, in most industries has a negative and/or statistically insignificant impact elasticity of sales. In some industries such as 04, 05, 07, 12, 13, and 16, the sales elasticity of non-production workers and inventories is not statistically different from zero. However, this is not as prevalent as in the case of capital stock. In some industries, such as electrical machinery and equipment and transportation equipment among the durables, and in petroleum and coal products among the nondurables, none of the stock variables is responsive, in the short run, to changes in sales. In almost all durable industries short-run sales elasticities of general utilization are about unity or close to it. However, in the nondurable industries, the short-run sales elasticities of Y_4, though very high, are below 1.

The evidence on the sales elasticity of the various inputs precludes any systematic ranking of the strength of the sales effect. In most of the nondurables the sales elasticities of the stock of inventories, Y_5, are fairly large in comparison with Y_1 and Y_2, while in the durable industries, Y_1 seems to be more responsive than the other dependent variables except Y_4. In some industries nonproduction workers, too, have fairly large sales elasticities.

b. Trend effects. Estimated trend coefficients are highly variable and often statistically insignificant. The utilization rate and production worker inputs almost always have negative trends, but no other patterns of trend sign emerge across industries. The magnitudes of trend co-efficients are generally smaller in the equations for capital stock and nonproduction worker employment.

c. Price elasticities. Few of the inputs in different industries show substantial price elasticities in the short run. In the durable industries, production worker employment is sensitive to price (w/c) in most cases, and in some durable industries the stocks of inventories and non-production worker employment also display statistically significant price elasticity. Hours worked have nonzero short-run price elasticity in electrical machinery (04), stone (08), and other durables (09). On the whole, Y_3, capital stock, shows very little short-run response to changes in relative prices in durable goods industries. Generally, the signs of the price coefficients across the durable industries are negative for labor equations and positive for capital stock equations. The signs of this variable in the general utilization and inventory equations do not follow consistent patterns and are often statistically insignificant. In most of the nondurable industries, production workers, hours, inventories, and utilization rates display significant short-run price responses. Non-production workers are also sensitive to changes in prices in some industries—paper (13), chemicals (14), petroleum (15), and other nondurables (17)—while capital stock is relatively price-elastic in industry 13 only. Thus, labor stocks and hours worked often have expected signs and statistically significant price elasticities in individual industries: occasionally inventories and the utilization rate also show some price sensitivity. Capital stock, on the other hand, almost always has a zero price elasticity in the short run. However, in all cases the magnitudes of the price responses are quite small.

iii. Own Adjustments

As noted before, own-adjustment coefficients, i.e., $1 - \hat{b}_{ii}$ in equation (4.1), must be positive and less than 1. Also, we expect own adjustments of utilization rates to be greater than those of stock variables. Table 6.18 indicates estimated own-adjustment coefficients in each industry. Several observations can be made about these estimates.

The generalized utilization rate, Y_4, is truly variable. Its own-adjustment coefficient is very close to unity in all cases. The own adjustment of hours of work, Y_2, varies across industries. On the whole, its adjustment coefficients have fairly high values and are larger than those for the labor stock variables. Also, hours tends to adjust slightly faster in the non-durable than in the durable industries. Capital stock, Y_3, shows the lowest adjustment coefficient, ranging from about 0.04 to 0.14 among the durables and from 0.0 to 0.10 among the nondurables. It is interesting to note that there are no significant differences in magnitude among both groups of industries. In contrast, nonproduction workers, Y_6, shows very high own-adjustment coefficients in most nondurable industries but much lower responses in durable goods industries. No significant pattern of own-adjustment coefficients emerges for production workers, Y_1. However, it should be noted that in nonautomotive transport (07) and petroleum (15) the coefficient of production workers is exceedingly large. Finally, in most industries, but especially in nondurables, the own-adjustment coefficient of the stock of inventories, Y_5, is more rapid than

TABLE 6.18

OWN-ADJUSTMENT COEFFICIENTS OF DEPENDENT VARIABLES IN INDIVIDUAL
MANUFACTURING INDUSTRIES[a]

				Durables					Industries					Nondurables		
Variables	01	02	03	04	05	06	07	08	09	10	11	12	13	14	15	16	17
Y_1	.47	.84	.54	.21	.52	.64	.02	.42	.41	.40	.47	.70	.31	.29	.06	.40	.39
Y_2	.30	.40	.62	.85	.28	.78	.28	1.0	.56	.40	.32	.71	.80	.54	.69	1.0	.11
Y_3	.12	.13	.09	.14	.09	.10	.12	.13	.04	.07	0.0	.08	.10	.07	.08	.07	.01
Y_4	.64	1.0	1.0	.51	1.0	1.0	1.0	1.0	1.0	.86	.63	1.0	1.0	1.0	.78	1.0	.76
Y_5	.40	.37	.20	.26	.31	.52	.25	.42	.72	.35	.90	.40	.71	.50	.53	.43	.37
Y_6	.19	0.0	.34	.06	.14	.36	.38	.67	.34	.07	.90	.68	1.0	.09	.33	.61	.24

a. These coefficients are calculated, from the own-regression coefficients in Tables 6.1 to 6.17, by deducting the value of the regression coefficients from unity. The industry codes are identified at the beginning of this chapter; the variables, in Table 6.17.

that of production workers. Most goods are made to order in durable goods industries and this result may reflect that practice. This issue will be discussed later on.

iv. Cross Adjustments

The pattern of the cross adjustments among the variables shows evidence of substantial feedbacks in all industries. As must be expected, the magnitudes of these feedbacks differ from one industry to another. However, some regularities in these patterns should be noted. The pattern of cross effects among the variables as a whole suggests that: (a) stock variables tend to be "dynamic complements" in the adjustment process; (b) flow variables respond rapidly to changes in exogenous variables, signaling subsequent changes in stock variables; (c) feedbacks among the stock variables are not always symmetrical; and (d) most of the feedbacks seem to be linked through the stock of production workers.

The following are some salient features of these interrelationships:

a. The disequilibrium effect of excess demand for production workers is mostly channeled through stock variables in various industries. It occurs infrequently. When it does its impact on the flow variables, Y_2 and Y_4, is positive and large, and concentrated mainly on Y_4. Note that the feedbacks between Y_1 and Y_2 are all concentrated among the durables and, except for food and beverages (11), this feedback does not occur among the nondurables.

b. The main effect of disequilibrium in hours worked falls on the demand for production workers, Y_1, in the equation for all industries, on nonproduction workers, Y_6, in durables, and on the level of inventories, Y_5, in nondurables. Disequilibrium in hours worked also has significant impacts, however, on generalized utilization rates, Y_4, and tends to be dynamically complementary with it.

c. Disequilibrium in capital stock, Y_3, affects production workers mainly in nondurables. It has a complementary relationship with nonproduction workers. Its effect on hours of work is concentrated mostly among the nondurables and on the generalized utilization rate among the durables.

d. Disequilibrium in the generalized utilization rate mainly increases demand for production workers and inventories. There is also some feedback from the excess demand for Y_4 on capital stock in several industries, and very few cases of feedbacks from disequilibrium in Y_4 on the other rate of utilization, Y_2, and the stock of nonproduction workers. The negative feedback from disequilibrium in Y_4 on demand for production workers is concentrated in the nondurables. The effect of excess demand for Y_4 on the level of inventories is mainly positive, suggesting that excess demand for Y_4 increases stocks of inventories. As the rate of capital utilization rises, demand for inventories increases as well. There is no observable effect on capital stock and nonproduction workers. The absence of feedback between Y_4 and Y_2 in most industries suggests that both may be responding to changes in stocks or variations in the exogenous variables.

e. Excess demand for inventories positively affects the demand for production workers and the rate of utilization of capital in almost all industries. The strongest effect falls mainly on demand for Y_4, and then on Y_1. There is evidence of some positive effect, mainly in the durable goods industries, of excess demand for inventories on demand for hours. Only a few cases of feedbacks of disequilibrium in inventory holdings on demand for stocks of capital and nonproduction workers are observed.

f. The cross effects of excess demand for nonproduction workers are mainly centered on demand for capital stock, Y_3, and the rate of utilization, Y_4. Excess demand for Y_6 decreases demand for investment in all industries where significant cross effects are present, durable goods in particular. In half of the durable goods industries, excess demand for nonproduction workers leads to decreases in both stocks of production workers and levels of inventories. In the nondurables this relationship is negative and occurs very infrequently.

The importance of cross adjustments in factor demand functions is summarized in Table 6.19. Entries in the table show the percentage of statistically significant cross effects (i.e., $\hat{b}_i$) of each variable in each industry, derived from Tables 6.1–6.17. Each variable can have a maximum of five statistically significant interactions. The numbers in each cell are the actual number of significant coefficients divided by 5.0. The numbers in the last row give the fraction of significant cross effects of all variables in each industry. The last column indicates the fraction of significant cross effects of each input across industries.

Though the pattern of cross effects varies across industries, the following general observations are warranted: Production worker employment and hours (Y_1 and Y_2) have the highest number of cross effects, while the

TABLE 6.19

FREQUENCY OF STATISTICALLY SIGNIFICANT CROSS EFFECTS OF MODEL (4.1) FOR INDIVIDUAL MANUFACTURING INDUSTRIES[a]

(per cent)

Variables	Industries															Percentage Frequency Across All Industries[b]
	Durables									Nondurables						
	02	03	04	05	06	07	08	09	11	12	13	14	15	16	17	
Y_1	0.6	.6	.2	.2	.8	.8	0.8	.6	.8	.8	.8	.4	.6	.4	0.6	.60
Y_2	1.0	.4	.6	.6	.8	.8	0.2	.2	.6	.4	.4	.4	.6	.8	1.0	.58
Y_3	0.2	.2	.2	.2	.4	.4	0.8	.8	.8	.8	.8	.4	.6	.2	0.6	.49
Y_4	0.2	.8	.4	.2	.4	.6	0.4	.2	.6	.2	.6	.2	.4	.6	0	.38
Y_5	0.4	.6	.8	.2	.4	.2	1.0	.4	.4	.2	.6	.2	0	.6	.2	.41
Y_6	1.0	.6	.4	.2	.2	.2	0.4	.6	.2	.6	.6	.8	0	.6	.6	.46
All inputs[c]	0.57	.53	.43	.27	.50	.50	0.60	.47	.57	.50	.63	.40	.37	.53	0.50	.50

a. The industry codes are identified at the beginning of this chapter; the variables, in Table 6.17.
b. Fraction of significant cross effects of each input across all industries.
c. Fraction of significant cross effects of each industry across inputs.

generalized rate of utilization, Y_4, and inventories, Y_5, have the lowest. In addition, there is no significant difference between the relative frequencies of durable and nondurable industries.

In conclusion, the results of cross-adjustment effects indicate that (i) feedbacks are important; (ii) the model captures them quite well; (iii) their patterns and directions differ, depending on the types of variable and industry characteristics involved; and (iv) there are strong "dynamic" complementarities and substitution relations among the stock variables. The own- and cross-adjustment effects for each industry imply corresponding distributed lag patterns and long-run elasticities for each variable.

B. DYNAMIC PROPERTIES

i. Distributed Lags

Transient response patterns of the variables to a unit of sales input are calculated for each industry in the manner described in Chapters 2 and 3. The distributed lag responses of the variables to changes in relative prices are ignored because the impact coefficients are numerically small and often statistically insignificant. In order to highlight the comparisons, we first concentrate on total durables and total nondurables; then we present the results for the individual industries.

Distributed lag patterns for the two aggregate industry groups are exhibited in Figures 6.1 and 6.2. On the whole, lags in durable and nondurable industries trace the same pictures as described above for total manufacturing. Utilization rates (Y_2 and Y_4) are the first and most rapidly adjusting inputs, particularly the generalized utilization rate. They overshoot their long-run values within three quarters after the shock and resume their most rapid movements back toward stationary values within seven quarters. Among stock variables, production worker employment (Y_1) adjusts most rapidly, followed by nonproduction workers and inventories. Capital stock is the slowest-adjusting input, tracing the characteristic "bell" pattern noted above for total manufacturing. There is no evidence of overshooting for production workers and capital stock, but there is some for nonproduction workers and inventories.

Generally speaking, the response patterns of total nondurables are displaced one or two quarters in time compared with total durables. More specifically, the responses of nondurables production worker

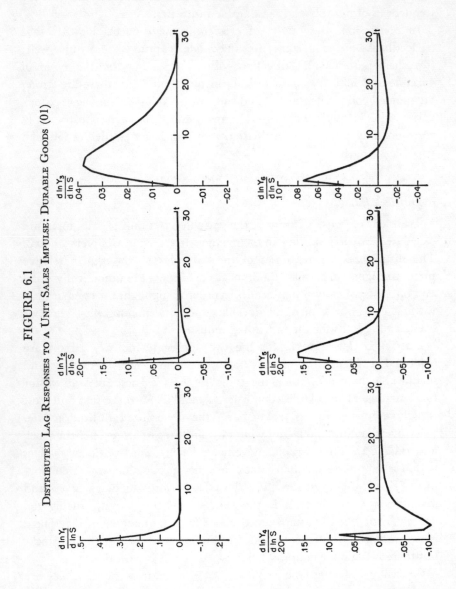

FIGURE 6.1

DISTRIBUTED LAG RESPONSES TO A UNIT SALES IMPULSE: DURABLE GOODS (01)

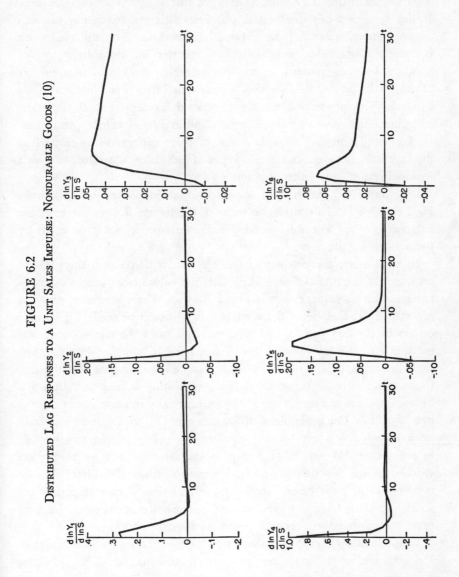

FIGURE 6.2

DISTRIBUTED LAG RESPONSES TO A UNIT SALES IMPULSE: NONDURABLE GOODS (10)

141

employment and hours worked lag behind the corresponding measures in durables by one quarter. Other stock variables (Y_3, Y_5, Y_6) in non-durables lag behind their counterparts in durables by at least two quarters. Initial responses are most often positive, with the exception of non-durable inventories and nonproduction workers. For all the stock variables, magnitudes of response are greater for durables than for nondurables. Lag patterns of most nondurable stock variables exhibit "thick" tails, accounting for similar patterns in total manufacturing as a whole. This property is most pronounced for capital stock, followed by nonproduction worker employment, and to a lesser extent, production worker employment. An explanation of these differences is related to the inventory decisions in the two types of industries, a subject to which we shall return in the next chapter.

Distributed lag patterns of the individual industries are shown in Figures 6.3–6.13. In contrast to most of the figures above, the response patterns here are not normalized. Hence, long-run elasticity is given by the area under the curve.

In most cases, the production worker distribution shows the greatest responses in the first and second period; the values often overshoot long-run equilibrium values except in four industries, where geometric patterns are traced. The mode of the distribution of hours worked (Y_2) always occurs in the first period, and in almost all cases the curve overshoots its final equilibrium value within a few periods after the impulse. On the other hand, capital stock (Y_3) exhibits a bell-shaped pattern although, in some industries, it is heavily skewed, exhibiting a thick tail. In a few industries, there are oscillatory patterns, especially in petroleum and coal products (15). The generalized utilization rate (Y_4) is the most regularly behaved variable, overshooting equilibrium values within two periods in every case. Inventories (Y_5) display the same pattern as production workers except that they are more dispersed in time. Slight irregularities are present in some cases. Finally, nonproduction worker responses are similar to those of inventories, though somewhat more regular. In most cases there is overshooting eight quarters after the shock.

In four industries, three of them nondurable, the model fails to depict the responses of the variables in a meaningful manner. The industries are transportation equipment excluding motor vehicles (07), chemical and allied products (14), food and beverages (11), and rubber products (16). In the first two, the dynamic system is stable, that is, the largest character-

FIGURE 6.3

DISTRIBUTED LAG RESPONSES TO A UNIT SALES IMPULSE: PRIMARY IRON AND STEEL (02)

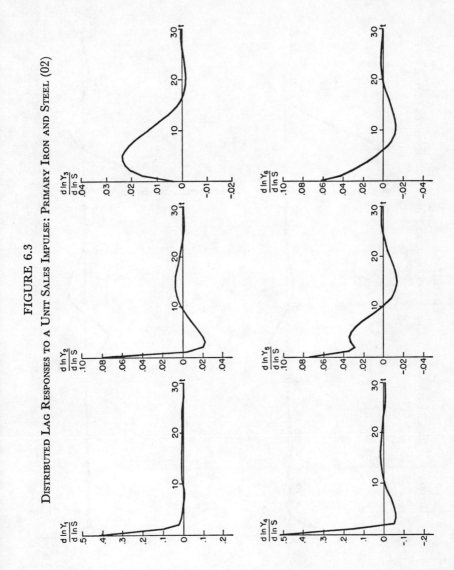

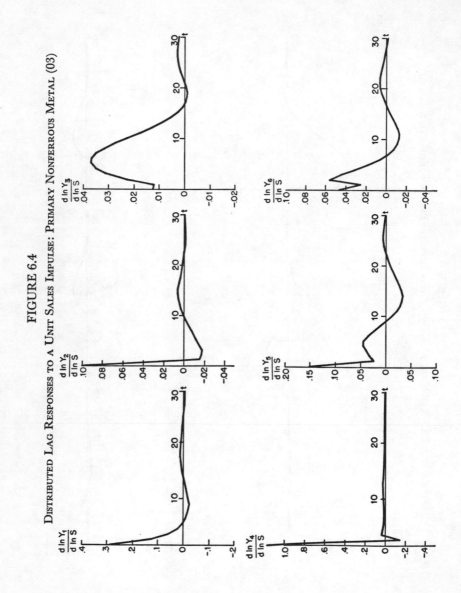

FIGURE 6.4

DISTRIBUTED LAG RESPONSES TO A UNIT SALES IMPULSE: PRIMARY NONFERROUS METAL (03)

144

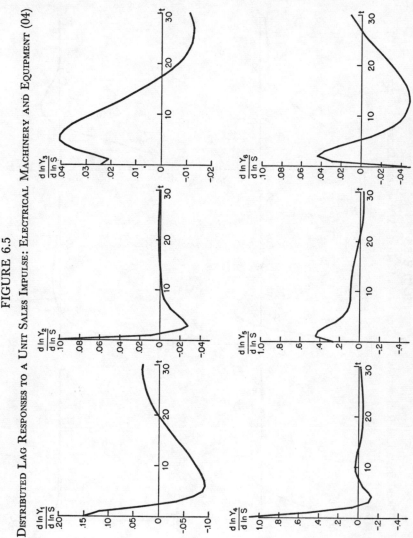

FIGURE 6.5

DISTRIBUTED LAG RESPONSES TO A UNIT SALES IMPULSE: ELECTRICAL MACHINERY AND EQUIPMENT (04)

145

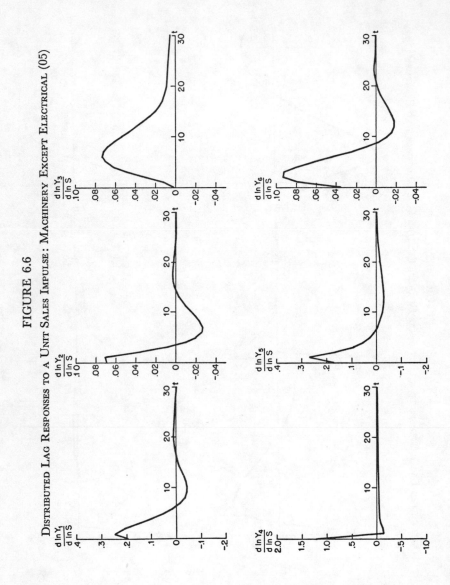

FIGURE 6.6

DISTRIBUTED LAG RESPONSES TO A UNIT SALES IMPULSE: MACHINERY EXCEPT ELECTRICAL (05)

146

FIGURE 6.7

DISTRIBUTED LAG RESPONSES TO A UNIT SALES IMPULSE: MOTOR VEHICLES AND EQUIPMENT (06)

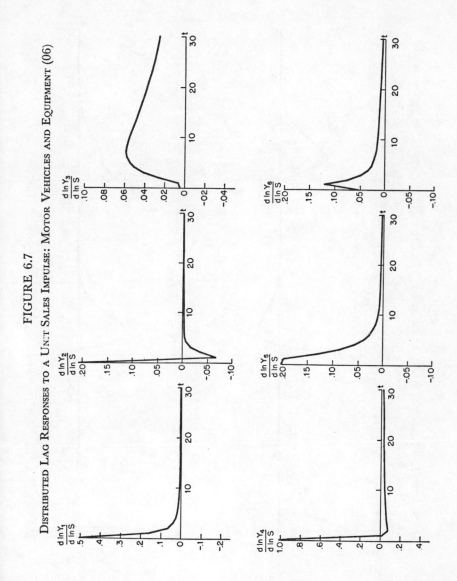

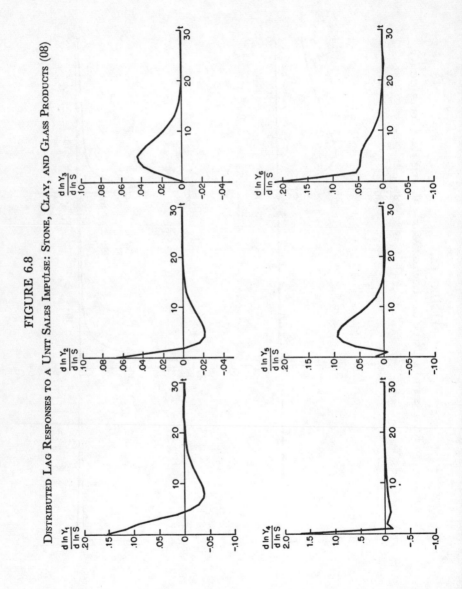

FIGURE 6.8

DISTRIBUTED LAG RESPONSES TO A UNIT SALES IMPULSE: STONE, CLAY, AND GLASS PRODUCTS (08)

148

FIGURE 6.9

DISTRIBUTED LAG RESPONSES TO A UNIT SALES IMPULSE: OTHER DURABLES (09)

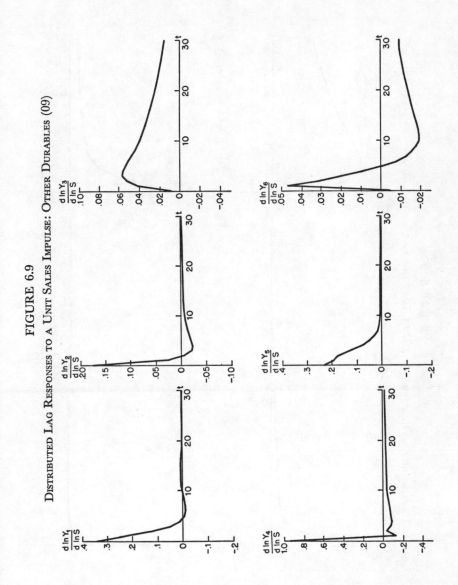

FIGURE 6.10

Distributed Lag Responses to a Unit Sales Impulse: Textile Mill Products (12)

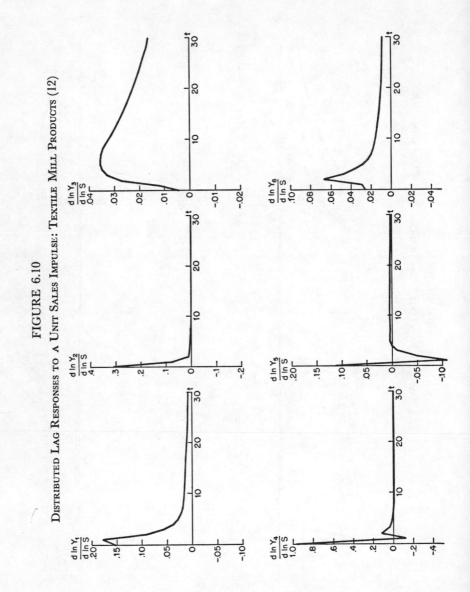

FIGURE 6.11

DISTRIBUTED LAG RESPONSES TO A UNIT SALES IMPULSE: PAPER AND ALLIED PRODUCTS (13)

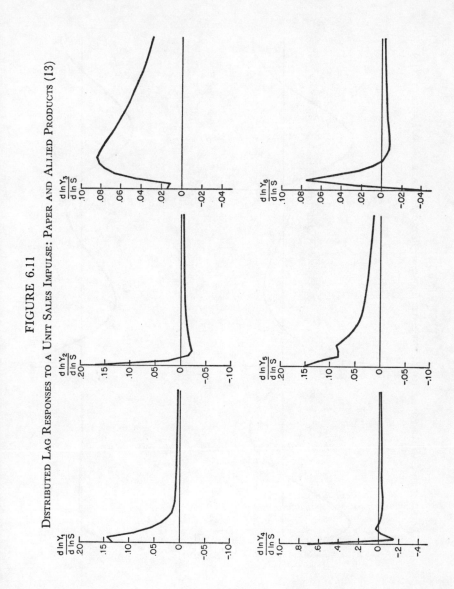

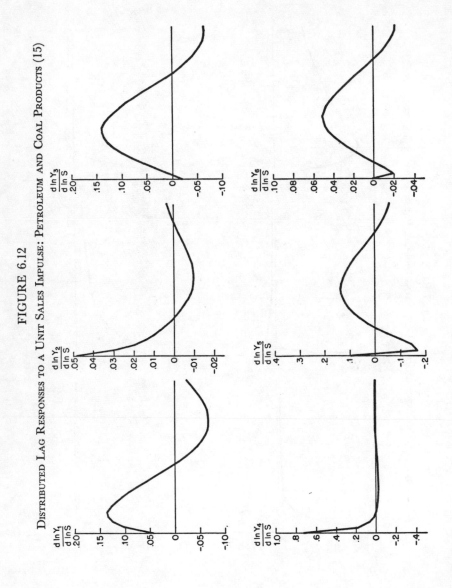

FIGURE 6.12

DISTRIBUTED LAG RESPONSES TO A UNIT SALES IMPULSE: PETROLEUM AND COAL PRODUCTS (15)

152

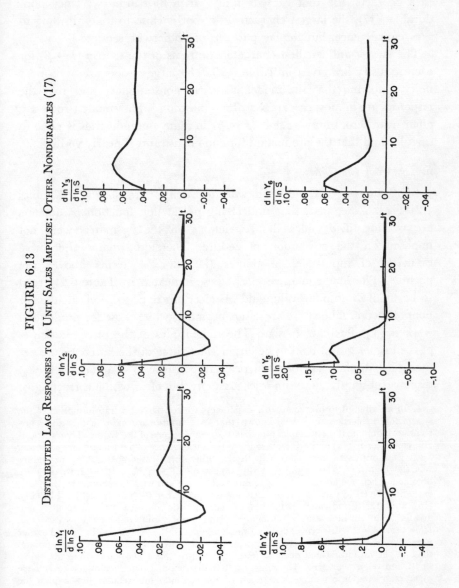

FIGURE 6.13

DISTRIBUTED LAG RESPONSES TO A UNIT SALES IMPULSE: OTHER NONDURABLES (17)

153

istic root of $(I - \beta)$ is less than 1, but the implied lag patterns are erratic and economically meaningless. In (11) and (16) the system explodes, that is, a characteristic root exceeds unity. In a fifth industry, other non-durables (17), the largest characteristic root is close to unity, leading to slow convergence, but the lag patterns are otherwise sensible.[1]

The largest and smallest characteristic roots of the matrix $(I - \beta)$ for each industry are given in Table 6.20. The largest roots are often near unity, implying that the model is nearly nonstationary and that the responses are in most cases of very long duration.[2] The smallest roots are often near zero, implying that $(I - \beta)$ in many subindustries is close to singular and that the production function constraint is nearly verified.

ii. Long-Run Elasticities

Long-run price, trend, and sales elasticities are shown in Tables 6.21–6.23. Note, first, that underlying production function parameters are overidentified, since the restrictions on the β_{ij} matrix were not imposed on the estimation procedure. Therefore, many alternative estimates of input-sales elasticities (i.e., the α_i terms above) are possible. The long-run price elasticities, indicated in Table 6.21, tend to be small in absolute value and of uncertain sign. Price elasticities for nonproduction labor (Y_6) are often negative, while those for production workers (Y_1) fluctuate in sign. The magnitudes of the price elasticities of the former group tend to be larger than those of the latter. Hours per man (Y_2) displays no long-run price responsiveness. Capital stock (Y_3) displays substantial long-run price elasticity, but often with incorrect signs,

1. In an attempt to overcome this deficiency, we considered a transformation of the system for these cases. It is well known that in nonstationary cases, a first-difference transformation of all the variables often leads to convergence of the system. This is especially called for in (11) and (16), where there is clear evidence of a nonstationary response. Such transformations may also help in the other three cases noted. Our procedure was the following: To begin, first differences of all variables (in logarithms) were obtained. Then a generalized least-squares technique was used to estimate model (4.1), excluding the trend variable. This procedure was performed for industries (07), (11), (14), (16), and (17). In no case was the largest characteristic root of the transformed system greater than 0.8, indicating a stationary response and rapid convergence as expected. However, two main differences between these results and the "stable results" noted earlier were apparent: First, there were more negative real roots in the first-difference estimates than in the untransformed ones; second, the long-run sales elasticities were extremely small and often near zero. This suggests that the first-difference technique to achieve a stationary response removes too much of the common interrelationships among the variables, and that other avenues need exploration.

2. When the model was estimated in the first-difference form for troublesome cases, the nonstationary aspect of the estimates disappeared in all cases.

TABLE 6.20

LARGEST AND SMALLEST CHARACTERISTIC ROOTS[a]
OF $(I-\beta)$ MATRIX, BY INDUSTRY

	Industries	Smallest Root	Largest Root
01	Total durables	.1572	.8919
02	Primary iron and steel	.1288	$.8544 \pm .2197i$
03	Primary nonferrous metal	−.1167	$.8625 \pm .2575i$
04	Elect. machinery and equip.	.1513	$.9454 \pm .1309i$
05	Machinery exc. elect.	.0453	.9016
06	Motor vehicles and equip.	.0587	.9608
07	Transport. equip. excl. motor vehicles		$(.7369 \pm .2456i)$
08	Stone, clay, and glass	−.0194	.8631
09	Other durables	−.1516	.9548
10	Total nondurables	.0520	.9827
11	Food and beverages		(.8403)
12	Textile mill products	.1081	.9665
13	Paper and allied products	−.0937	.9546
14	Chemical and allied products		(.7108)
15	Petroleum and coal products	.1049	$.9493 \pm .1536i$
16	Rubber products		(.6154)
17	Other nondurables	.1300	.9970

a. The figures shown in parentheses refer to the largest root of the first-order transformed version of the model.

especially in durable goods industries. The price effects of the general utilization rate are smaller in magnitude and opposite in sign to those for capital stock. Finally, inventories show negative price responses in durables and positive responses in nondurables. In summary, price responses in disaggregated industries exhibit some of the same undesirable features noted for total manufacturing and probably for the same reasons.

The trend elasticities vary in sign and magnitude among the variables and across industries. They have consistent negative signs only for production worker employment. Often, positive signs can be observed for Y_2, Y_3, Y_5, and Y_6, suggesting some misspecification of the trend term as a proxy for technical changes, a phenomenon noted above. Again, overidentification is relevant in this connection.

The sales elasticities are the largest in magnitude of the three exogenous variables. They also vary greatly, both among variables and across different industries. Sales "returns to scale" indicate increasing returns for durables except nonelectrical machinery (05), motor vehicles (06), and other durables (09), and decreasing returns for the nondurables. The long-run effect of sales on hours worked is consistently zero, as expected, but the effect on general utilization rates is highly variable. Long-run scale effects show large variations for stock variables across industries and from one stock input to another. Indeed, some signs are

TABLE 6.21

LONG-RUN PRICE ELASTICITIES, BY INDUSTRY

	Inputs					
Industries[a]	Prod. Emp. (Y_1)	Hours (Y_2)	Capital (Y_3)	Util. (Y_4)	Inven. (Y_5)	Nonprod. Emp. (Y_6)
01	.0186	.0438	−0.0349	−.5215	−.0316	−.1676
02	−.2055	.1175	−0.3721	.1240	−.1787	−.3350
03	.2024	.0820	−0.3158	.2420	−.8256	−.1508
04	.2568	.0572	−0.3159	.0342	−.0144	−.2186
05	−.2364	.0301	−0.3643	−.1075	.5909	−.3264
06	.0953	.1178	1.0156	−.9694	−.0659	.3893
07[b]						
08	−.1354	−.0051	−0.0093	.1924	−.2689	−.0085
09	.0009	.0105	0.1683	−.2696	−.0857	−.3022
10	.0455	.0177	0.0589	.0536	.0125	.0244
11[b]						
12	−.0688	−.0454	0.1391	−.0721	.2208	.0025
13	−.0543	−.0597	0.1725	−.2374	.1805	−.1203
14[b]						
15[b]						
16[b]						
17	−.2840	−.0112	−0.9888	.1266	−.0777	−.4744

a. The industry codes are identified in Table 6.20.
b. Long-run effects could not be computed because the adjustment matrix was not stable (largest root exceeded 1).

TABLE 6.22

LONG-RUN TREND ELASTICITIES, BY INDUSTRY

	Inputs					
Industries[a]	Prod. Emp. (Y_1)	Hours (Y_2)	Capital (Y_3)	Util. (Y_4)	Inven. (Y_5)	Nonprod. Emp. (Y_6)
01	−.0037	.0006	.0062	−.0085	.0042	.0066
02	−.0051	.0015	.0033	.0028	.0062	.0000
03	−.0005	.0006	.0047	−.0079	.0056	.0022
04	.0158	−.0001	.0080	−.0232	.0281	.0129
05[b]						
06	−.0087	.0002	−.0021	−.0003	.0145	−.0001
07[b]						
08	.0002	.0015	.0056	−.0009	.0031	−.0008
09	−.0044	.0001	.0031	.0010	−.0018	.0085
10	−.0158	−.0008	−.0220	−.0132	−.0033	−.0095
11[b]						
12	−.0065	−.0032	.0055	−.0102	.0100	.0032
13	−.0041	.0012	−.0074	.0033	−.0042	.0087
14[b]						
15[b]						
16[b]						
17	−.0189	−.0012	−.0752	−.109	−.0154	−.0296

a. The industry codes are identified in Table 6.20.
b. Long-run effects could not be computed because the adjustment matrix was not stable (largest root exceeded 1).

negative, especially for Y_6, which is certainly unacceptable. Further, the large size of the sales elasticities for other nondurables (17) is undoubtedly due to its nearly nonstationary response.

In attempting to account for these results, the most likely explanation, in addition to overidentification of the relevant parameters, runs as follows: We are trying to make inferences about long-run response patterns on the basis of estimates that reflect one-period changes in (quarterly) data. Thus, the estimates of βA_1 in the computation of long-run elasticity estimates are regression coefficients from *current* values only of the exogenous variables, while the estimates of $[I - (I - \beta)]^{-1}$ stem from *one*-period lags of the dependent variables. Any small variations in the regression estimates can become magnified greatly in computing long-run coefficients. Though such a result is not a *necessary* consequence of estimating the elements of $(I-\beta)$ and βA_1 from current and one-period changes, it does become a very important factor when the convergence of the system is very slow, and that is what the characteristic roots of Table 6.20 indicate.

The homogeneous part of any system of linear difference equations can be expressed in the form

$$Y_{it} = c_{1i}\lambda_1^t + c_{2i}\lambda_2^t + \ldots,$$

where the c_{ij} terms are constants, and the λ's are characteristic roots of $(I - \beta)$. In the estimates above, the largest root is greater than 0.95. Thus, for example, only after about 40 periods (10 years!) does the term in the above expression containing $\lambda > 0.95$ contribute as little as 0.20

TABLE 6.23

LONG-RUN SALES ELASTICITIES, BY INDUSTRY

	Inputs					
Industries[a]	Prod. Emp. (Y_1)	Hours (Y_2)	Capital (Y_3)	Util. (Y_4)	Inven. (Y_5)	Nonprod. Emp. (Y_6)
01	0.7052	.0016	0.4112	0.5442	0.6455	0.1007
02	0.5778	.0101	0.2238	0.4229	0.2052	0.0970
03	0.4514	.0439	0.3846	0.1353	0.1589	0.1959
04	−0.3130	.0073	0.3082	0.9085	2.506	−0.3872
05	0.7363	.0310	0.8899	0.3756	0.3410	0.4071
06	1.091	.0245	1.853	−0.5940	0.9748	0.8116
07[b]						
08	0.1355	−.0583	0.3627	0.4489	0.6995	0.7448
09	0.8344	−.0635	1.308	−0.6239	1.031	−0.4238
10	2.063	.1178	3.474	1.436	1.219	1.694
11[b]						
12	1.049	.3538	1.232	0.8423	0.1229	0.7411
13	0.7144	−.1523	2.191	−0.3914	1.627	−0.0429
14[b]						
15[b]						
16[b]						
17	4.494	0.3701	17.26	−0.0327	3.982	7.080

a. The industry codes are identified in Table 6.20.

b. Long-run effects could not be computed because the adjustment matrix was not stable (largest root exceeded 1).

to the time path of Y_{it} [i.e., $(0.96)^{40} = 0.20$]. Thus, it is the *combination* of factors that makes accurate estimation of long-run elasticities very difficult: First, the regression estimates are computed from very short-run changes; second, the dynamic stability of the estimates is nearly non-stationary (i.e., the absolute value of at least one root is close to unity). Again, errors in computing the tail of the distributed lag are *cumulative* in estimating long-run effects. If, in fact, the system converged more rapidly, such errors would be small, and more reliable inferences about long-run scale and substitution effects could be made.

C. SUMMARY

Though the estimated structural coefficients, distributed lags and long-run elasticities vary from industry to industry and a considerable range of issues has been covered, the main results of our analysis of the individual industries can be summarized.

i. Short-run properties of the model are very satisfactory. The estimates and distributed lag properties confirm the existence of significant feedbacks among the inputs. The fit and forecast properties of the model are excellent.

ii. There are significant differences between the durable goods and nondurable goods industries, with few intragroup differences present.

iii. The long-run elasticity estimates in some industries could not be computed. However, we should underscore the fact that consistency of the short- and long-run elasticities is a difficult test for any model to pass. In most other comparable models, this vexing problem of consistency has been simply assumed away.

7

FURTHER OBSERVATIONS, SUMMARY, AND CONCLUSIONS

IN this final chapter, we first comment on interindustry results reported in previous chapters and then compare our results with those reported in the literature. An over-all summary and conclusion is contained in section C.

A. INTERINDUSTRY DIFFERENCES

Impact effects, distributed lags, and long-run coefficients show substantial variation among industries, reflecting corresponding variation in industrial structure. Many of the systematic patterns among the results were noted above and need not be repeated. Instead, we concentrate on the three salient features of the results: (i) Response patterns for nondurable industries are slower and displaced one or two quarters behind those in durables; (ii) long-run sales responses tend to be much greater in durables, in contrast to long-run price effects, which are similar and small among all industries; (iii) distributed lag patterns do not converge in several nondurable industries.

An explanation for these divergences must be sought in the underlying characteristics of the two types of industry. Sales and price variability as measured by the coefficient of variation is much higher in durables than in nondurables. Furthermore, as measured by wage rates, workers in the durables industries tend to be more skilled and, also, more highly unionized (Lewis [1963]). The fraction of woman workers is much greater in nondurables than in durables, and turnover rates tend to be slightly higher in these industries. Finally, as indicated in Appendix B, Tables B.1 to B.5, utilization rates are significantly higher in nondurables over the sample period, in part because of the lower variation in output and the manner in which utilization is measured. All these factors suggest that input responses should be *slower* in durables than in nondurables. Yet the reverse behavior is observed.

One clue toward resolution of the issue is provided by the large differential impact effect of sales on inventories between industries. The immediate inventory response is strong and positive for most durable industries, but strongly negative for most nondurables. This difference might be due to differences in the composition of total inventories (Y_5) between groups. Finished goods constitute about 50 per cent of total inventory in nondurable manufacturing, but only about 33 per cent in durables (*Survey of Current Business*). Purchased materials constitute about 30 to 35 per cent of total inventories in both. However, the main difference is in the relative proportions of goods in process. For example, in total durables it is about 40 per cent of the total, while in total nondurables it is about 13–15 per cent of the total. These breakdowns suggest that in durables the initial impact of a change in sales is mainly borne by finished goods inventories, but in durables, by all types of inventory, and especially goods in process. Finished goods evidently serve as a better buffer against sales fluctuations in nondurables, which exhibit smaller relative sales variations. Finished goods inventories are likely to be relatively interchangeable with "inventories" of productive inputs, whereas goods in process are more likely to be complementary to other factors of production. Inventories of finished goods provide a wedge between sales variations and input decisions. In contrast, goods in process do not serve this function. Hence, input decisions can be delayed in industries where the proportion of finished goods inventories is higher, that is, in nondurable industries. These relationships imply relatively stronger and direct linkages between inventories and productive inputs in the case of durables, forcing more rapid adjustments of inputs to changes in sales in those industries.[1]

Some further evidence is provided by the relative behavior of unfilled orders and new orders in the two types of industry. Both mean and relative

---

1. It can be argued that if the inventory-sales ratio is high, the buffer function of inventories should be greater, independently of composition. This ratio is higher for durables than nondurables in our data and seemingly goes against the argument in the text. However, note that this ratio is not an exogenous variable in our model and may merely reflect the same kinds of forces underlying the delayed adjustment as those already mentioned.

variance of unfilled orders is much higher in durables than in nondurables (see Tables B.1 and B.4 in Appendix B). Large backlogs reflected by unfilled orders in durables are in fact a type of inventory "held" by *buyers* rather than sellers. These "inventories" arise because a large fraction of durables manufacture is made to order, to the technical specifications of the buyer. These goods are "thinly" traded, because of their technical specificity. On the other hand, backlog "inventories" in nondurable industries are extremely small, because these goods are homogeneous and easily marketed. These technological differences link sales and production decisions and hence input decisions more closely in durables than in nondurables.

We conclude that this relation between inventory and sales variability is stronger than and outweighs higher "adjustment costs" in durables in linking input decisions over time. Therefore, input lags to sales shocks are shorter in durable goods. These same factors also contribute to lack of convergence of estimated responses in some nondurable industries. Note that production function restrictions have not been imposed a priori on the estimates. In most cases the smallest characteristic root is near zero, implying that the restrictions come close to being fulfilled. It still remains true that the production function is overidentified. If the restrictions held identically, and the scale parameters were exactly identified, the result—that returns to scale are much higher in durable goods industries than in nondurables—would reinforce our interpretation of the response patterns described above, namely, if returns to scale are sharply diminishing, firms will not find it optimal to adjust output very rapidly. As it stands, the estimated long-run sales elasticities can only be suggestive in this regard.

B. COMPARISONS WITH THE LITERATURE: EMPIRICAL RESULTS

As mentioned in Chapter 2, the model underlying this study is a generalization of existing employment investment functions. It presents new evidence on the interpretation of short-term employment and investment functions obtained by less general methods.

It was noted in Chapter 1 that previous short-run employment functions yielded implausibly high short-run returns to scale to labor inputs and exceedingly long lags of adjustment (Brechling [1965], Jorgenson [1963]). There are two possible explanations for these results in the context of the present model.

First, if one takes the fixed output constraint of the production function seriously, there is a good possibility that observed long adjustment lags of labor may really be only "sympathetic" reflections of long lags elsewhere in the system. In model (4.1) this possibility is allowed for by specifying the interdependence of adjustment lags among all inputs. Thus, if capital stock or nonproduction employment or both are the real sources of adjustment delays in the system, all other inputs will reflect the long lags of these two factors as a matter of course, because the output or sales constraint must be maintained during the adjustment period. Indeed, that is one of the major empirical findings of the present study. Most of the lag distributions on capital stock are of the familiar "bell" pattern and imply exceedingly long response lags. On the other hand, most of the responses of production employment and utilization rates tend to overshoot their long-run equilibrium values fairly soon after the shock, so that the sales-production function constraints are maintained while capital changes. Use of the Koyck or stock adjustment formulation in the absence of interaction terms simply precludes the possibility of ever estimating response patterns of the sort we found above, and such restrictions are clearly unwarranted. Thus, the small stock adjustment coefficients estimated in most time-series employment models really do not reflect costly labor adjustment alone, but also adjustment costs elsewhere in the system, and therefore have no ready interpretation. It must be noted, however, that in those studies using disaggregated data for the United States, adjustment delays in nondurable industries tend to be longer than those in durables (Dhrymes [1969]), a finding also derived in the present study.

Secondly, model (4.1) allows us to perform certain conceptual experiments that are capable of generating all possible short-run input demand functions, depending on what factors are considered to be "fixed" in the short run. Since our initial four-equation model (Nadiri and Rosen [1969]) using labor and capital stocks and utilization rates and real output rather than sales is more comparable with models in the literature than with our expanded model, these experiments were first performed with the former estimates.

i. The labor stock adjustment model considered in the literature can be approximated arbitrarily in our larger model by conceptually fixing Y_3 (capital stock) and Y_4 (general utilization) in the short run and treating them as parameters and ignoring inventories and nonproduction labor.

This reduces the model to a two-equation interrelated model in labor stock and labor utilization. On the basis of our earlier results, estimated short-run output elasticities under this procedure are 1.36 for employment stock (Y_1) and 0.12 for hours per man (Y_2). Hence, estimated returns to scale for employment equal $1/1.36 = 0.735$, suggesting decreasing returns, as is indicated in the theory; and these values are far below most of the usual ones estimated, which typically range above unity. To approximate returns to "scale" for total man-hours, output coefficients of Y_1 and Y_2 may be added, resulting in estimated short-run returns to scale for total labor input of 0.68.

ii. If capital services are allowed to vary by fixing capital stock only (Y_3), the conceptual experiment is performed by working with a three-equation interrelated model in Y_1, Y_2, and Y_4. These three equations are used to solve for the stationary values of Y_1, Y_2, and Y_4 in terms of output (Q), w/c, T, and Y_3. Now output elasticities are estimated as 0.77 for Y_1, 0.14 for Y_2, and 0.81 for Y_4. Estimated returns to scale are 1.30 for Y_1, and 1.10 for man-hours of production workers.

Taken at face value, these experiments suggest the following conclusion. The reason for large returns to scale, for labor estimated from short-run employment functions is that the rate of utilization of capital is omitted. These high estimates should not be considered as returns to labor alone, but are interpreted more properly as short-run returns to both labor and capital utilization. We note that similar conclusions have been reached in a more recent discussion of the issue, though from a rather different approach (Ireland and Smyth [1967]).

Similar experiments were performed with the full model aggregate estimates for total manufacturing (Table 4.1) and are presented in Table 7.1. The equations corresponding to the inputs considered "variable" for experimental purposes were solved for steady state values in terms of sales, w/c, T, and the inputs considered "fixed," as in the experiment above. Thus, the first line gives the results for a two-equation subsystem; the second line, for a three-equation subsystem; and so on. The results from the first two lines are very similar to the results reported above for the simpler four-equation full-model estimates: decreasing returns to production labor if capital utilization is considered to be "fixed," and increasing returns if it is considered to be "variable." There are still "increasing returns" to labor as inventories (line 3) and finally nonproduction labor are allowed to "vary"; these too must be considered as factors accounting for estimated short-run increasing returns to labor in previous short-run employment studies.

Generally speaking, according to the Le Chatelier principle, when some of the inputs are assumed to be fixed, the estimated "stationary" responses, shown in Table 7.1, of the "variable" inputs should be greater than the "fixed" variables when all factors are free to vary (given the sales constraint). The long-run elasticities of the full model based on Table 4.1 were 0.73 for Y_1, $- 0.130$ for Y_2, 1.20 for Y_4, 0.177 for Y_5, and 0.156 for Y_6. Comparing these figures with those of Table 7.1, it is seen that the expectation is usually borne out for Y_2, Y_4, Y_5, and Y_6. On the other hand, it is true for Y_1 only in the first experiment.

Some qualifications to these results should be kept in mind:

i. These experiments are truly conjectural in nature, since model (4.1) stresses the dynamic interrelationships of all factors. In our model, all inputs are specified as "quasi-fixed," and none of them are really entirely fixed in the "short run." Thus, arbitrarily fixing some inputs for the purpose of the exercise is, strictly speaking, outside the framework of the model. Yet the procedure is suggested for purposes of comparison with existing models and to highlight the fact that most of the short-run employment functions are implicitly based on such assumptions.

ii. Also, there is some arbitrariness in the experiment because the restrictions on the β_{ij} adjustment terms are not met exactly and the production

TABLE 7.1

"Short-Run" Scale Effects, Production Worker Employment, and Hours of Work in Total Manufacturing, Full Model[a]

	Inputs Considered	Inputs Considered	Estimated Scale Effects				
Line	Variable	Fixed	Y_1	Y_2	Y_4	Y_5	Y_6
1	Y_1, Y_2	Y_3, Y_4, Y_5, Y_6	1.08	.33	—	—	—
2	Y_1, Y_2, Y_4	Y_3, Y_5, Y_6	0.68	−.09	1.24	—	—
3	Y_1, Y_2, Y_4, Y_5	Y_3, Y_6	0.74	−.04	0.91	.33	—
4	Y_1, Y_2, Y_4, Y_5, Y_6	Y_3	0.47	−.22	2.00	.05	.53

a. Derived from estimates in Table 4.1.

function is overidentified. This means that more than one estimate of the production function parameters is possible. For example, in experiment (i) above in the four-equation model any two equations can be deleted to solve for Y_1 and Y_2 in terms of output, and so on at stationary values. That is, choose any two equations, set $Y_{it} = Y_i$ for all i, and solve the two equations simultaneously for Y_1 and Y_2 in terms of Y_3, Y_4, and so on. If the constraints hold and the production function is identified exactly, any pair will produce the same estimate of short-run returns to scale. We chose the first two as being more in the "spirit" of the employment function literature, but some other result would be obtained by using some other pair. Similar remarks hold for experiment (ii) and for those in Table 7.1.

iii. We have already noted the difficulty of estimating long-run coefficients in models of this sort in the face of the nearly nonstationary response of the dynamic system and the relatively short period (20 years) spanned by available data. That discussion applies equally to other studies.

The main import of investment functions in the literature can be summarized as follows: (a) Distributed lag patterns display long lags of adjustment and tend to be "bell" shaped; (b) estimated long-run relative price elasticity has considerable range, depending on the a-priori restrictions used in estimation (Jorgenson and Siebert [1968], Jorgenson and Stephenson [1967]); and (c) the output elasticity is also subject to great variation, depending on specification. Our model throws new light on all these issues.

We could have performed conceptual experiments similar to those above. Our capital stock structural equation contains the previous period's utilization, employment, and inventory variables, in contrast to the neoclassical investment functions, which usually do not include such variables. Had we ignored these feedbacks, geometric distributed lag investment functions would have been obtained. However, when the full set of feedbacks is included, bell-shaped patterns emerge. This result was obtained for all industries without the a-priori restriction of imposing second-order lag terms on the structure. In contrast to the results reported by Jorgenson and Stephenson [1967], who constrain initial responses of investment to changes in output and prices to be zero immediately following the shocks, we find immediate nonzero responses in most industries. The result is that the mode of the lag distributions is about four quarters shorter than that obtained by Jorgenson and Stephenson. As in their results for some industries, we find oscillatory behavior far out in the tail of the investment-sales distribution. However, the industries where the oscillations occur are not the same in the two studies.

In the neoclassical investment models developed by Jorgenson [1963], Jorgenson and Stephenson [1967], and Bischoff [1971], there is evidence of substantial long-run price response to investment. We do not find such evidence. In the majority of cases, our price elasticities for capital as well as most other inputs are quite small. The estimates are very close to those reported by Eisner and Nadiri [1968] and Mayor [1971]. One reason for the difference is that our estimates are not tied to output responses as in the Bischoff and Jorgenson models. Another reason is that the impact price effects in our model are quite small. This, in conjunction with the slow convergence of the system, makes estimation of the long-run price effects difficult. Finally, the difference may be in using different measures of relative prices. We use wage-rental ratios whereas Jorgenson uses real rental prices. Different sample periods and data have been used in each study as well.

Finally, we do not find any evidence of constant return to scale, which is in contrast to the practice of imposing that restriction on the estimates a priori. Our result is in conformity with those obtained in time-series production function studies (Nerlove [1967b]).

C. SUMMARY AND CONCLUSIONS

In this study we have attempted to formulate and estimate a fully integrated model of demand for factors of production. The principal feature of this model lies in its disequilibrium character, corresponding to a generalized interrelated stock adjustment model. The effect of disequilibrium in one input spills over to the adjustments of all inputs, resulting in a network or feedback mechanism that traces the dynamic properties of the inputs over time. The potential of the model lies in integrating and presenting a generalized framework for time-series study of production, employment, investment, and utilization behavior. The model lends itself to certain economically meaningful conceptual experiments: (i) The passage of a unit impulse of an exogenous variable through the system generates various distributed lag patterns for all inputs, which take into account all cross adjustments and interactions among them. (ii) The stationary values of the inputs resulting from step function impulses are equivalent to conventional long-run scale and substitution effects in the theory of supply.

A specific form of the general model has been specified and estimated from quarterly time-series data for manufacturing industries in the post-World War II period. The investigation is confined to six inputs: production and nonproduction employment, hours of work, capital stock, generalized utilization, and total inventories. The coverage of the study includes total manufacturing, total durables and nondurables, and fifteen manufacturing industries for which the necessary data could be obtained. The driving forces in a dynamic system such as ours depend on the number and character of the exogenous variables in the structural estimates, sales, trend, and the wage-rental ratio. Data limitations preclude incorporating other relevant factors, such as other input prices, rental price of labor, and so forth.

Experiments with empirical estimation of the model have been confined to various specifications at the aggregate, total manufacturing level. These include (i) various "shock" specifications for both realized and anticipated sales and relative prices and (ii) examination of the stochastic structure of the model, including own- and cross-serial correlation to the extent possible. The results of these experiments indicate that current sales and current relative prices perform as well if not better than their "expected" counterparts. Furthermore, there is reason to prefer estimation techniques that account for first-order serial correlation in the disturbances. A first-order Cochran-Orcutt transformation on each equation is used for this purpose. The final model includes current sales, current relative prices, and trend in a system of first-order difference equations with a Cochran-Orcutt transformation of residuals for each equation. This model is used to estimate the structural parameters for the disaggregated industries and for forecasting beyond the sample period (1968I–1970II) for total manufacturing, total durables, and total nondurables.

Reduced form parameters of the model can be obtained by recursive methods from structural parameters. We also estimated certain reduced form parameters directly (for total manufacturing), and the results are comparable with those implied by the structural estimates.

The over-all estimates can be summarized as follows:

i. On the whole, the model fits the data exceedingly well on both aggregate and disaggregated levels. Goodness-of-fit statistics suggest its superiority in the sample period to a series of autoregressive models. Many alternative models have failed to pass this test.

ii. Forecast properties of the model were very satisfactory in the three industry aggregates—total manufacturing, total durables, and total nondurables—for which forecasts outside the sample period could be carried out. Forecasts were particularly good for levels of stock variables, as measured by size of forecast errors and turning points. The model tended to track hours per man with a one-period lag, reflecting the actual one-period lead of hours per man over other inputs. Generalized utilization rate forecast errors were large because the method of calculating the series imposed an upper limit of 100 per cent.

iii. Impact or first-period responses of sales tended to follow a systematic pattern in all industries. The effects were largest for utilization rates, but significantly smaller for stock variables. Production worker responses displayed the biggest impact effects among the stock variables and capital stock the smallest. Impact effects of relative factor prices were quite small in most cases, but were often statistically significant, especially in the labor and capital utilization equations. Estimated coefficients of trend were small in magnitude and showed no systematic patterns of statistical significance in different inputs and various industries.

iv. Structural estimates strongly confirm the disequilibrium specification of the model, which is its major innovative feature. Strong feedback effects are indicated by highly significant regression estimates on most lagged dependent variables in each equation and in each industry. In most industries excess demand for production workers tends to increase hours of work per man and utilization of capital, but decreases the demand for inventories, nonproduction workers, and capital stock. In most cases, excess demand for hours per man has a strong negative feedback on both labor stock variables and much weaker effects on the other inputs. Excess demand for capital stock tends to decrease production and nonproduction worker employment and inventories and to increase utilization rates. Disequilibrium in capital utilization positively affects demand for capital stock and inventories and negatively affects demand for production workers; it exhibits no effect on demand for hours and nonproduction workers. On the whole, excess demand for inventories increases demand for other inputs. Finally, excess demand for nonproduction workers tends to decrease demand for production workers, hours worked, and capital stock; it has no predictable effect on level of inventories and rate of utilization. These feedback effects display some tendency toward symmetry, in that excess demand for input i affects the demand for input j in the same direction as excess demand for input j affects demand for input i. However, the tendency is weak, and many exceptions to this general statement can be found.

v. The distributed lag or the transitory response to changes in sales indicate very interesting results: (a) Utilization rates respond first and most quickly, transmitting the shock effect to the stock variables; (b) production workers follow utilization rates in terms of the speed of response; (c) nonproduction workers and inventories are rather slow in response to sales shocks; and (d) capital stock exhibits the slowest response pattern of all inputs. This pattern of response of the inputs suggests a similar rank ordering of variables in terms of ease of adjustment or an inverse rank ordering in terms of "fixity."

Most remarkably, the utilization rates and, to a lesser extent, production worker employment tend to *overshoot their equilibrium values* in almost all industries, a result that cannot be estimated in any other comparable model. Capital stock and, to a lesser extent, inventories and nonproduction workers exhibit a bell-shaped distribution often found for capital stock in other studies. The significance of these overshooting patterns for utilization rates should be emphasized, for they constitute the major justification for disequilibrium models and have significant economic meaning. To maintain sales targets, the more easily adjustable inputs, viz., utilization rates and production workers, are allowed to exceed equilibrium values to give the firm time to adjust the more fixed and costly inputs. Moreover, no evidence of zero initial response was found. All these *general* properties of the distributed lag patterns noted are extraordinarily insensitive to different specification and estimation procedures, strengthening our confidence in these findings.

vi. Systematic differences in the response patterns were found between durable and nondurable industries. The speed of response is slower in the nondurables and the convergence to equilibrium values is less rapid than in durables. In many of these cases characteristic roots of the system had imaginary parts resulting in minor damped oscillations far out in the tails of the lag distributions. The model fails to converge in some of the disaggregated industries, mainly in nondurables. Convergence in these explosive cases can be obtained by prefiltering the data through first-difference transformations. However, such transformations force very rapid convergence of the system and cause oscillations due to negative real characteristic roots. These cases need further exploration.

vii. Long-run coefficients tended to suggest significant differences in returns to scale between durables and nondurables, the latter exhibiting decreasing returns and the former increasing returns. However, the magnitudes of these estimates were highly sensitive to minor changes in specification. The reason for this lies in the convergence properties of the system. Often the lag distributions on which these estimates are based display "thick" tails, making interpretation of the results difficult. The distributed lags are nearly nonstationary. We found no systematic evidence on price and trend elasticities for the dependent variables.

viii. The model integrates empirical employment and investment functions and consequently can be used to generate estimates comparable to those found in the literature. A set of conceptual experiments was used to generate short-term employment functions. It was found that the high short-run returns to labor observed in most studies was probably due to omission of capital utilization. Long employment and hours adjustment lags, often found in such studies, are undoubtedly due to long adjustment lags elsewhere in the system, such as in capital stock. No evidence of constant returns to scale was found for capital stock, and price elasticity was always small in absolute value and often of the wrong sign. It should be noted that the bell-shaped distributed lag pattern of capital was obtained from a first-order system and not from second-order own lags in the capital stock equation. The modes of these lag distributions fell around three to four quarters after the initial impact.

Though we hope that some problems in time-series factor demand functions have been resolved by this study, other difficulties remain. Further attention needs to be given to the following problems: (i) Essentially, there exists at present no genuine market theory of supply in a dynamic setting. A complete theory is needed to resolve simultaneously the interactions between optimum expectations and reactions of individual producers in a market setting. (ii) More attention should be given to improving the quality and sources of data. Specifically, there is great need for better capital utilization and price data. (iii) Finally, better estimation techniques for dealing with serial correlation in dynamic time-series models are needed. This is especially so in view of the slow convergence of these systems.

APPENDIXES

APPENDIX A

INDUSTRIAL CLASSIFICATION

Nadiri-Rosen Code	Industry	U.S. Standard Industrial Classification (SIC)
00	Total manufacturing	
01	Total durables	
	Ordnance and accessories	19
	Lumber and wood products	24
	Furniture and fixtures	25
	Stone, clay, and glass products	32
	Primary metal industries	33
	Fabricated metal products	34
	Machinery, except electrical	35
	Electrical equipment and supplies	36
	Transportation equipment	37
	Instruments and related products	38
	Miscellaneous manufacturing industries	39
02	Primary iron and steel	
	Blast furnace and basic steel products	331
	Iron and steel foundries	332
03	Primary nonferrous metal	333
	Secondary nonferrous metals	334
	Nonferrous rolling and drawing	335
	Nonferrous foundries	336
	Miscellaneous primary metal products	339
04	Electrical machinery and equipment	36
05	Machinery except electrical	35
06	Motor vehicles and equipment	371
07	Transportation equipment excluding motor vehicles	
	Aircraft and parts	372
	Ship and boatbuilding and repairing	373
	Railroad equipment	374
	Other transportation equipment	375, 379

175

Nadiri-Rosen Code	Industry	*U.S. Standard Industrial Classification (SIC)*
08	Stone, clay, and glass products	
09	Other durables	
	Ordnance and accessories	19
	Lumber and wood products	24
	Furniture and fixtures	25
	Fabricated metal products	34
	Instruments and related products	38
	Miscellaneous manufacturing industries	39
10	Total nondurables	
	Food and kindred products	20
	Tobacco manufactures	21
	Textile mill products	22
	Apparel and other textile products	23
	Paper and allied products	26
	Printing and publishing	27
	Chemicals and allied products	28
	Petroleum and coal products	29
	Rubber and plastics products	30
	Leather and leather products	31
11	Food and beverages	20
12	Textile mill products	22
13	Paper and allied products	26
14	Chemical and allied products	28
15	Petroleum and coal products	29
16	Rubber products	30
17	Other nondurables	
	Tobacco manufacture	21
	Apparel and other textile products	23
	Printing and publishing	27
	Leather and leather products	31

APPENDIX B

DESCRIPTIVE STATISTICS OF QUARTERLY TIME SERIES FOR INDIVIDUAL INDUSTRIES AND INDUSTRY AGGREGATES

TABLE B.1

Descriptive Statistics of Quarterly Time-Series Data for Total Durables, Primary Iron and Steel, and Primary Nonferrous Metal

(sample period: 1953I–1967IV)

Variables[a]	Total Durables (01)			Primary Iron and Steel (02)			Primary Nonferrous Metal (03)		
	Mean	Stand. Dev.	Coeff. of Var. $\times 100$	Mean	Stand. Dev.	Coeff. of Var. $\times 100$	Mean	Stand. Dev.	Coeff. of Var. $\times 100$
Y_1	7.289	0.6126	8.405	0.718	0.076	10.580	0.311	0.025	8.030
Y_2	40.841	0.8132	1.991	39.995	1.511	3.777	41.478	0.994	2.390
Y_3	40.656	8.484	20.868	8.155	0.657	8.050	4.341	0.624	14.370
Y_4	0.8989	0.834	9.283	0.778	0.147	18.890	0.791	0.101	12.760
Y_5	30.826	7.429	24.103	3.407	0.512	15.020	1.984	0.383	19.300
Y_6	2.190	0.492	22.475	0.145	0.009	6.200	0.083	0.006	7.220
S	47.651	10.800	22.665	5.479	1.064	19.410	3.488	0.601	17.230
w	2.194	0.486	22.137	2.789	0.405	14.510	2.566	0.389	15.170
c	0.1164	0.035	29.940	0.131	0.028	21.445	0.131	0.028	21.445
P	0.9323	0.114	12.289	0.968	1.004	10.369	1.024	0.059	5.803

a. For description and units of measure, see Table 3.1.

TABLE B.2

Descriptive Statistics of Quarterly Time-Series Data for Electrical Machinery and Equipment, Machinery Except Electrical, and Motor Vehicles and Equipment

(sample period: 1953I–1967IV)

Variables[a]	Electrical Machinery and Equipment (04)			Machinery Except Electrical (05)			Motor Vehicles and Equipment (06)		
	Mean	Stand. Dev.	Coeff. of Var. × 100	Mean	Stand. Dev.	Coeff. of Var. × 100	Mean	Stand. Dev.	Coeff. of Var. × 100
Y_1	1.031	0.134	12.990	1.115	0.121	10.850	0.596	0.080	13.422
Y_2	40.400	0.546	1.350	41.798	1.043	2.490	41.767	1.534	3.672
Y_3	3.427	0.607	17.710	6.346	1.330	20.950	5.835	0.731	12.527
Y_4	0.901	0.086	9.540	0.841	0.096	11.410	0.811	0.139	17.139
Y_5	5.709	0.909	15.920	5.377	1.785	33.190	2.483	0.586	23.600
Y_6	0.448	0.100	20.490	0.453	0.065	14.340	0.169	0.012	7.100
S	7.153	1.533	21.431	6.723	1.953	29.040	8.311	1.958	23.559
w	2.245	0.317	14.125	2.542	0.383	15.069	2.798	0.453	16.183
c	0.131	0.028	21.445	0.131	0.028	21.445	0.131	0.028	21.445
P	0.965	0.052	5.385	1.006	0.113	11.258	0.973	0.059	6.156

a. For description and units of measure, see Table 3.1.

TABLE B.3

Descriptive Statistics of Quarterly Time-Series Data for Transportation Equipment Excluding Motor Vehicles; Stone, Clay, and Glass; and Other Durables

(sample period: 1953I–1967IV)

Variables[a]	Transportation Equipment Excluding Motor Vehicles (07)			Stone, Clay, and Glass (08)			Other Durables (09)		
	Mean	Stand. Dev.	Coeff. of Var. × 100	Mean	Stand. Dev.	Coeff. of Var. × 100	Mean	Stand. Dev.	Coeff. of Var. × 100
Y_1	0.649	0.100	15.408	0.489	0.016	3.271	2.485	0.149	5.995
Y_2	41.107	0.702	1.707	41.062	0.646	1.573	40.562	0.617	1.521
Y_3	2.436	0.770	31.600	4.270	0.768	17.985	9.467	1.402	14.809
Y_4	0.889	0.068	7.649	0.927	0.059	6.364	0.942	0.050	5.307
Y_5	4.807	0.817	16.996	1.342	0.271	20.193	8.633	0.909	10.529
Y_6	0.314	0.036	11.464	0.109	0.013	11.926	0.692	0.100	14.450
S	5.080	0.865	17.027	2.752	0.437	15.879	12.509	1.786	14.277
w	2.642	0.423	16.010	2.259	0.334	14.779	2.173	3.146	14.482
c	0.131	0.028	21.445	0.131	0.028	21.445	0.131	0.028	21.444
P	0.9884	0.073	7.376	0.993	0.060	6.048	1.002	0.053	5.255

a. For description and units of measure, see Table 3.1.

TABLE B.4

DESCRIPTIVE STATISTICS OF QUARTERLY TIME-SERIES DATA FOR
TOTAL NONDURABLES, FOOD AND BEVERAGES, AND TEXTILE MILL PRODUCTS
(sample period: 1953I–1967IV)

Variables[a]	Total Nondurables (10)			Food and Beverages (11)			Textile Mill Products (12)		
	Mean	Stand. Dev.	Coeff. of Var. × 100	Mean	Stand. Dev.	Coeff. of Var. × 100	Mean	Stand. Dev.	Coeff. of Var. × 100
Y_1	5.705	0.1755	3.0765	1.224	0.056	4.575	0.872	0.075	8.600
Y_2	39.5275	0.4529	1.1460	41.045	0.266	0.6480	40.068	1.180	2.944
Y_3	49.1691	6.2173	1.2645	9.167	0.232	2.530	3.472	0.324	9.331
Y_4	0.9517	0.049	5.1746	0.960	0.036	3.750	0.948	0.053	5.590
Y_5	20.4499	3.7226	18.2034	5.655	0.671	11.865	2.427	0.318	13.102
Y_6	1.66811	0.2295	13.7611	0.565	0.029	5.132	0.092	0.006	6.521
S	42.5308	9.095	21.3850	15.804	2.138	13.528	3.685	0.639	17.340
w	1.8727	0.3948	21.0846	2.076	0.342	16.478	1.625	0.214	13.171
c	0.1164	0.0348	29.9402	0.131	0.028	21.445	0.131	0.028	21.445
P	0.9887	0.0400	4.051	1.001	0.031	3.128	1.011	0.031	3.098

a. For description and units of measure, see Table 3.1.

TABLE B.5

DESCRIPTIVE STATISTICS OF QUARTERLY TIME-SERIES DATA FOR PAPER AND ALLIED PRODUCTS, CHEMICAL AND ALLIED PRODUCTS, AND PETROLEUM AND COAL PRODUCTS

(sample period: 1953I–1967IV)

Variables[a]	Paper and Allied Products (13)			Chemical and Allied Products (14)			Petroleum and Coal Products (15)		
	Mean	Stand. Dev.	Coeff. of Var. × 100	Mean	Stand. Dev.	Coeff. of Var. × 100	Mean	Stand. Dev.	Coeff. of Var. × 100
Y_1	0.476	0.024	5.042	0.526	0.026	4.942	0.138	0.020	14.492
Y_2	42.675	0.459	1.075	41.313	0.397	0.9609	41.382	0.608	1.469
Y_3	5.041	1.066	21.146	9.923	1.288	12.979	18.166	1.169	6.435
Y_4	0.964	0.036	3.734	0.962	0.036	3.742	0.967	0.032	3.309
Y_5	1.600	0.282	17.625	3.419	0.753	22.023	1.689	0.108	6.394
Y_6	0.119	0.019	15.966	0.315	0.047	14.920	0.071	0.002	2.816
S	3.825	0.692	18.091	6.967	1.731	24.845	4.138	0.422	10.198
w	2.250	0.366	16.271	2.459	0.399	16.217	2.883	0.403	13.969
c	0.131	0.028	21.445	0.131	0.028	21.445	0.131	0.028	21.445
P	0.9743	0.046	4.781	1.0019	0.026	2.587	1.009	0.054	5.385

a. For description and units of measure, see Table 3.1.

TABLE B.6

Descriptive Statistics of Quarterly Time-Series Data for Rubber Products and Other Nondurables

(sample period: 1953I–1967IV)

Variables[a]	Rubber Products (16)			Other Nondurables (17)		
	Mean	Stand. Dev.	Coeff. of Var. × 100	Mean	Stand. Dev.	Coeff. of Var. × 100
Y_1	0.312	0.043	13.782	2.111	0.084	3.979
Y_2	40.797	0.954	2.338	37.138	0.386	1.039
Y_3	1.555	0.248	15.948	4.303	0.444	10.318
Y_4	0.918	0.075	8.169	0.965	0.032	3.316
Y_5	1.062	0.195	18.361	6.160	0.619	10.048
Y_6	0.089	0.014	15.730	0.518	0.041	7.915
S	2.021	0.440	21.771	9.736	1.588	16.310
w	2.289	0.292	12.771	1.991	0.268	13.469
c	0.131	0.028	21.445	0.131	0.028	21.445
P	0.998	0.067	6.747	0.985	0.028	2.914

a. For description and units of measure, see Table 3.1.

APPENDIX C

ESTIMATED STRUCTURE OF THE MODEL

TABLE C.1

PREDICTIVE AND STRUCTURAL TESTS OF MODEL (4.1), TOTAL
MANUFACTURING, 1948I–1967IV AND 1968I–1970II

	Predictive Tests (F_p)	Structural Tests (F_S)
Y_1	0.7102	0.4975
Y_2	1.6982	1.0930
Y_3	0.3994	0.5491
Y_4	0.9311	0.5836
Y_5	0.7229	0.4986
Y_6	1.2835	1.0092

COMMENT: A comparison of F_p and F_S with their critical values (1.99 at the .05 level) suggests acceptance of the null hypothesis that the forecast errors are generated by model (4.1) and that no structural change occurred over the periods considered.

NOTE: The predictive and structural test statistics, F_p and F_S, were calculated as

$$F_p = \frac{V_1^2/m}{V_2^2/(n-k)} = \frac{e_0'[I + X_0(X'X)^{-1}X_0]^{-1}e_0/m}{e'e/(n-k)},$$

$$F_S = \frac{(X\beta_1 - X\beta_2)^2 + (Y_0 - X_0\beta_2)^2}{(Y - X\beta_1)^2}\frac{n-k}{k},$$

where V_1^2 and V_2^2 are the sums of squared errors for the forecast and sample periods; n and m are the number of observations in the sample and the forecast periods, respectively; k is the number of independent variables. Y is the vector of observations on the dependent variables and X is the matrix of observations

184

on k independent variables during the period of fit; while X_0 is a matrix of observations of the independent variable and Y_0 is the vector of the dependent variable for the period of forecast and β_1 and β_2 are the estimated coefficients of model (4.1) for the sample period and the whole period 1948I–1970II. The statistic F_S is an approximate test of structural change (see Johnson [1963], pp. 137–38 for further details).

TABLE C.2

ESTIMATED STRUCTURE OF MODEL (4.1) WITH FORECASTED SALES
VARIABLE (Z_1), TOTAL MANUFACTURING SECTOR

(sample period: 1948I–1967IV; all variables except trend are in natural logarithms)

Indepen- dent Variables	Dependent Variables					
	Prod. Emp. (Y_{1t})	Hours (Y_{2t})	Capital (Y_{3t})	Util. (Y_{4t})	Inven. (Y_{5t})	Nonprod. Emp. (Y_{6t})
Constant	−6.720 (6.559)	−.0008 (.0175)	.5990 (1.644)	.0909 (.8414)	−7.269 (3.137)	−.7155 (1.424)
Wage	−.0124 (.5070)	−.0201 (1.319)	−.0176 (.8655)	−.0009 (.1654)	−.0391 (.4266)	−.0254 (.8736)
Trend	−.0036 (4.966)	.0018 (2.280)	.0007 (1.447)	.0004 (2.612)	−.0032 (1.424)	.0012 (1.608)
Sales	.1855 (2.270)	.0010 (.8041)	−.0009 (.2419)	.0049 (.3646)	−.0384 (1.216)	−.0208 (4.095)
Y_{1t-1}	.5041 (6.754)	.0303 (.6144)	.0047 (.0854)	.0989 (6.076)	−.0436 (.1673)	.3211 (4.069)
Y_{2t-1}	1.674 (6.019)	.0982 (.8816)	.7529 (4.587)	−.0595 (1.126)	3.001 (3.870)	.6070 (2.600)
Y_{3t-1}	.3238 (3.726)	−.0250 (.2614)	−.0435 (.5872)	.9409 (41.07)	.2536 (.8063)	−.1033 (.9675)
Y_{4t-1}	−.1285 (3.096)	.0384 (2.534)	−.0491 (2.102)	−.0148 (2.265)	.0296 (.2413)	−.0924 (2.802)
Y_{5t-1}	−.0389 (.6340)	.0048 (.1345)	−.0083 (.1902)	.0153 (1.248)	−.6940 (3.350)	.6222 (9.926)
Y_{6t-1}	.0351 (.4606)	.7346 (8.102)	−.0352 (.5908)	−.0216 (1.303)	1.110 (4.143)	.3464 (4.037)
R^2	.9561	.9364	.5464	.9995	.6330	.9929
SEE	.0123	.0045	.0070	.0019	.0368	.0100
$\hat{\rho}$	.0261	.9187	.4975	.4975	.3093	.5141

TABLE C.3

Estimated Structure of Model (4.1) Without Utilization Rate (Y_4),
Total Manufacturing Sector

(sample period: 1948I–1967IV; all variables except trend are in natural logarithms)

Independent Variables	Prod. Emp. (Y_{1t})	Hours (Y_{2t})	Capital (Y_{3t})	Inven. (Y_{5t})	Nonprod. Emp. (Y_{6t})
Constant	−2.402 (2.905)	4.816 (7.964)	.2470 (1.198)	−.6588 (.5935)	−.9657 (1.814)
Wage	−.0140 (.5932)	−.0336 (2.055)	.0015 (.2965)	−.0240 (.8092)	−.0143 (.9395)
Trend	−.0044 (5.394)	.0014 (1.803)	.0002 (.6524)	.0010 (1.343)	.00008 (.1622)
Sales	.4470 (13.35)	.1892 (8.611)	−.0048 (.6935)	.0168 (.3421)	.0404 (1.848)
Y_{1t-1}	.4349 (6.933)	.0451 (.9700)	.0279 (1.738)	.2694 (3.380)	−.0032 (.0798)
Y_{2t-1}	.3652 (2.019)	−.2006 (1.715)	−.0022 (.0596)	.3519 (1.324)	.2530 (2.134)
Y_{3t-1}	.1835 (1.756)	−.2009 (2.187)	.8987 (26.63)	−.0918 (.8460)	.00002 (.0004)
Y_{5t-1}	.0020 (.0410)	−.0599 (1.665)	.0038 (.3263)	.6662 (10.54)	.0009 (.0296)
Y_{6t-1}	−.0689 (.8184)	−.1302 (1.576)	.1038 (3.279)	.2555 (3.142)	.9248 (18.07)
R^2	.9853	.9390	.9999	.9980	.9995
SSR	.0036	.0016	.0001	.0076	.0015
SEE	.0072	.0047	.0015	.0104	.0047
$\hat{\rho}$	.7295	.8803	.9516	.4853	.6985

TABLE C.4

ESTIMATED STRUCTURE OF MODEL (4.1) WITH FORWARD VALUES OF
SALES AND WAGES, TOTAL MANUFACTURING SECTOR

(sample period: 1948I–1967IV; all variables except trend are in natural logarithms)

Indepen-dent Variables	Dependent Variables					
	Prod. Emp. (Y_{1t})	Hours (Y_{2t})	Capital (Y_{3t})	Util. (Y_{4t})	Inven. (Y_{5t})	Nonprod. Emp. (Y_{6t})
Constant	−2.608 (2.907)	.9030 (2.507)	.0828 (.3598)	3.986 (1.603)	−.6967 (.5599)	−.0116 (.0203)
Wage	−.0182 (.6794)	−.0127 (.8213)	.0011 (.2100)	−.0863 (.9360)	.0220 (.5744)	−.0071 (.4534)
Trend	−.0051 (5.985)	−.0015 (7.213)	−.00002 (.0596)	−.0071 (4.443)	.0017 (1.629)	.0003 (.5191)
Sales	.4085 (10.91)	.0964 (3.446)	−.0048 (.6427)	1.060 (7.062)	−.0005 (.0098)	.0342 (1.638)
Y_{1t-1}	.4819 (7.764)	−.0821 (3.892)	.0488 (2.749)	−.2650 (1.736)	.2980 (3.544)	.0160 (.3896)
Y_{2t-1}	.4468 (2.009)	.7099 (7.479)	.0329 (.7320)	−.2061 (.3119)	.6219 (1.958)	−.0086 (.0676)
Y_{3t-1}	.1448 (1.417)	−.0137 (.4821)	.9116 (26.82)	−.2894 (1.402)	−.1596 (1.232)	−.0795 (1.031)
Y_{4t-1}	−.0251 (.9064)	−.0389 (2.566)	−.0114 (1.995)	.1307 (1.345)	−.1209 (2.997)	.0470 (2.985)
Y_{5t-1}	−.0357 (.5772)	−.0717 (3.725)	.0094 (.6585)	−.5533 (3.924)	.6903 (8.295)	.0332 (.8524)
Y_{6t-1}	.0065 (.0789)	.0717 (3.112)	.0805 (2.416)	.8861 (5.317)	.2840 (2.716)	.8385 (12.25)
S_{t+1}	.0730 (2.068)	.0807 (2.674)	.0071 (.9971)	.0088 (.0589)	.0367 (.7044)	.0358 (1.807)
S_{t+2}	−.0584 (1.473)	−.0643 (2.027)	−.0097 (1.229)	.1610 (.9984)	.0001 (.0030)	.0252 (1.137)
S_{t+3}	.0582 (1.554)	.0545 (1.779)	.0071 (.9470)	−.2653 (1.685)	−.0769 (1.393)	.0059 (.2848)
S_{t+4}	.0221 (.5599)	.0385 (1.843)	.0033 (.4067)	−.0215 (.1697)	−.0044 (.0785)	−.0154 (.6692)
w_{t+1}	−.0080 (.2988)	−.0071 (.3218)	−.0010 (.1825)	.1094 (.9747)	−.0667 (1.692)	−.0122 (.7924)
w_{t+2}	−.0260 (.9485)	−.0315 (1.387)	−.0005 (.0882)	−.0972 (.8508)	−.0022 (.0546)	−.0255 (1.630)
w_{t+3}	.0124 (.4654)	.0374 (1.741)	−.0039 (.7193)	.0349 (.3186)	.0122 (.3136)	−.0020 (.1333)
w_{t+4}	−.0107 (.4277)	−.0040 (.2838)	−.0076 (1.411)	−.0397 (.4668)	−.0112 (.3146)	−.0093 (.6320)
R^2	.9877	.9642	.9999	.9218	.9984	.9996
SSR	.0030	.0009	.0001	.0335	.0061	.0010
SEE	.0070	.0039	.0015	.0234	.0100	.0042
$\hat{\rho}$	.6305	−.2847	.9321	.0460	.5258	.8179

TABLE C.5

ESTIMATED STRUCTURE OF MODEL (4.1) WITH FORWARD VALUES OF
SALES, TOTAL MANUFACTURING SECTOR

(sample period: 1948I–1967IV; all variables except trend are in natural logarithms)

Independent Variables	Dependent Variables					
	Prod. Emp. (Y_{1t})	Hours (Y_{2t})	Capital (Y_{3t})	Util. (Y_{4t})	Inven. (Y_{5t})	Nonprod. Emp. (Y_{6t})
Constant	−2.594 (3.101)	1.166 (3.333)	.0206 (.0958)	3.942 (1.706)	−.9935 (.8425)	−.0157 (.0270)
Wage	−.0252 (1.030)	−.0245 (3.045)	.0015 (.2820)	−.0585 (1.044)	−.0056 (.1684)	−.0054 (.3612)
Trend	−.0052 (6.284)	−.0015 (6.891)	−.00008 (.2523)	−.0074 (4.872)	.0016 (1.556)	.0009 (1.004)
Sales	.4143 (11.67)	.1093 (4.029)	−.0043 (.5987)	1.085 (7.645)	−.0128 (.2424)	.0435 (2.214)
Y_{1t-1}	.4839 (7.953)	−.0762 (3.495)	.0503 (2.923)	−.2501 (1.677)	.2998 (3.588)	.0657 (1.406)
Y_{2t-1}	.3811 (1.817)	.6499 (6.869)	.0240 (.5691)	−.2444 (.3886)	.6160 (2.011)	−.1007 (.8801)
Y_{3t-1}	.1701 (1.829)	−.0344 (1.352)	.9187 (28.10)	−.2518 (1.426)	−.0996 (.8525)	−.0536 (.6047)
Y_{4t-1}	−.0178 (.6732)	−.0378 (2.455)	−.0103 (1.889)	.1185 (1.261)	−.1123 (2.850)	.0449 (3.010)
Y_{5t-1}	−.0517 (.9216)	−.0681 (3.628)	.0036 (.2731)	−.5939 (4.637)	.6609 (8.659)	.0388 (1.059)
Y_{6t-1}	.0142 (.1741)	.0671 (2.839)	.0854 (2.661)	.9202 (5.744)	.3003 (2.918)	.7121 (8.166)
S_{t+1}	.0677 (2.022)	.0698 (2.402)	.0069 (1.019)	−.0197 (.1377)	.0386 (.7698)	.0375 (2.012)
S_{t+2}	−.0443 (1.208)	−.0468 (1.551)	−.0081 (1.109)	.1488 (.9907)	.0252 (.4598)	.0366 (1.847)
S_{t+3}	.0629 (1.808)	.0512 (1.768)	.0087 (1.245)	−.2347 (1.603)	−.0837 (1.604)	.0106 (.5589)
S_{t+4}	.0163 (.4552)	.0310 (1.529)	.0075 (.9845)	−.0140 (.1188)	−.0150 (.2890)	−.0223 (1.078)
R^2	.9874	.9607	.9999	.9198	.9983	.9996
SSR	.0031	.0010	.0001	.0344	.0065	.0011
SEE	.0069	.0039	.0015	.0230	.0100	.0041
$\hat{\rho}$	.6563	−.2284	.9278	.0566	.5455	.9283

APPENDIX D

GLOSSARY OF IMPORTANT SYMBOLS

Symbol	Meaning
A_1	Matrix of fixed coefficients
B	Matrix of adjustment coefficients
c	User cost of capital (rental price of capital)
c_I	User cost of inventories
$g(\ )$	Cost of changing inputs
I^g	Gross investment expenditures in 1954 dollars
K_t	Stock of capital in 1954 dollars
k'	Tax credit rate
k_i	Constants
k	Number of independent variables
L	Lag operator
M	Matrix characteristic roots of vector of $(I - \beta)$
m_1	Mean error
m_2	Mean absolute error
m_3	Mean square error
N	New orders
n	Number of observations in the forecast period
ou	Stock of unfilled orders
P	Unit price of output
P_k	Unit purchase price of capital stock
$(\ )^P$	"Permanent" component
Q	Level of output
q	Vector of exogenous variables ($y_t^* = A_1 q_t$)
q_p	Quit rate

Symbol	Meaning
R	Vector of relative input prices
r	Rate of interest (cost of capital)
S	Sales (shipments) in constant dollars
s_n	User cost of nonproduction worker
s_p	User cost of production worker
$(\ )^T$	"Transitory" component
T	Trend
V_p	Hiring cost per worker
W	Wealth
w_n	Hourly wage of nonproduction man-hours
w_p	Hourly wage of production man-hours
x	Level of output in constant dollars
Y_1	Stock of production workers
Y_2	Hours of work per production worker
Y_3	Capital stock (constant 1954 dollars)
Y_4	Rate of capital services per unit of capital stock
Y_5	Stock of inventories
Y_6	Stock of nonproductive workers
Y_7	Hours of work per nonproductive worker
Y_i^*	Desired input level
$\hat{Y}_i$	Forecast values of Y_i; $i = 1, \ldots, 6$

Symbol	Meaning	Symbol	Meaning
$\hat{\bar{Y}}_i$	Mean of $\hat{Y}_i$	ε	Stochastic error term
$\bar{Y}_i$	Mean value of the dependent variable in the forecast range	ε'	Stochastic error term
		λ	Characteristic roots of $(I - \beta)$
y_t	Inputs	$\Theta(L)$	Polynomial function of L
Z	Predicted sales	$\Theta_{ij}(L)$	Polynomial function of L
z	Present value of depreciation	μ_i	Vector of fixed depreciation rates
α_i	Cobb-Douglas exponents (output elasticities)	μ_0	Stochastic error term
β	Coefficient of adjustment	ν	Vector of nominal input prices
β_{ij}	Matrix of adjustment coefficients	ξ'	Elasticities of wage rate with respect to hours worked
γ	Return to scale parameter	ρ	First-order serial correlation coefficient
δ	Capital depreciation rate	ω	Corporate income tax rate

APPENDIX E

REFERENCES

Alchian, A. "Information Costs, Pricing and Resource Unemployment." In Phelps et al. [1970].

Anderson, W. H. L. *Corporate Finance and Fixed Investment*. Boston, Graduate School of Business Administration, Harvard University, 1964.

Arrow, K. J. "Price-Quantity Adjustments in Markets with Rising Demands." In K. Arrow, S. Karlin, and P. Suppes, eds. *Mathematical Methods in the Social Sciences, 1959*. Stanford, Calif., Stanford University Press, 1960, pp. 3–15.

Arrow, K. J., S. Karlin, and H. Scarf. *Studies in the Mathematical Theory of Inventory and Production*. Stanford, Calif., Stanford University Press, 1958.

Ball, R., and E. St. Cyr. "Short-Term Employment Functions in British Manufacturing Industry." *Review of Economic Studies* 33 (July 1966): 179–208.

Bischoff, C. W. "Lags in Fiscal and Monetary Impacts on Investment in Producers' Durable Equipment." Presented at the Conference on the Effect of Tax Incentives on Investment, Washington, D.C., Brookings Institution, 1967. Processed.

———. "Business Investment in the 1970's: A Comparison of Models." *Brookings Papers on Economic Activity*, Vol. 1, no. 1. Washington, D.C., 1971.

Black, S. W., and H. H. Kalejian. "A Macro Model of the U.S. Labor Market." *Econometrica* 38 (September 1970): 712–741.

Board of Governors of the Federal Reserve System. *Federal Reserve Bulletin*. Various issues.

Bodkin, R., and L. Klein. "Nonlinear Estimation of Aggregate Production Functions." *Review of Economics and Statistics* 49 (February 1967): 28–44.

Brainard, W., and J. Tobin. "Pitfalls in Financial Model Building." *American Economic Review* 58 (May 1968): 99–122.

Brechling, F. P. R. "The Relationship Between Output and Employment in British Manufacturing Industries." *Review of Economic Studies* 32 (July 1965): 187–216.

Brechling, F. P. R., and P. O'Brien. "Short-Run Employment Functions in Manufacturing Industries: An International Comparison." *Review of Economic Statistics* 49 (August 1967): 277–287.

Bry, G. *The Average Workweek as an Economic Indicator,* New York, NBER, 1959. Reprinted in G. H. Moore, ed. *Business Cycle Indicators,* Vol. I. New York, NBER, 1961.

Chetty, V., and U. Sankar. "On the Specification of Distributed Lags." 1967. Processed.

Christ, C., "Aggregate Econometric Models." *American Economic Review* 46 (June 1956): 385–408.

Cochrane, D., and G. H. Orcutt. "Application of Least Squares Regressions to Relationships Containing Auto-Correlated Error Terms." *Journal of the American Statistical Association* 44 (March 1949): 32–61.

Denison, D. F. *The Sources of Economic Growth in the United States and the Alternatives Before Us.* New York, Committee for Economic Development, 1962.

Dhrymes, P. "A Model of Short-Run Labor Adjustment." In J. Duesenberry et al., eds. *The Brookings Model: Some Further Results.* Chicago, Rand-McNally, 1969.

Dhrymes, P., and M. Kurz. "Technology and Scale in Electricity Generation." *Econometrica* 32 (July 1964): 287–315.

Duesenberry, J. *Business Cycles and Economic Growth.* New York, McGraw-Hill, 1958.

Eisner, R. "A Distributed Lag Investment Function." *Econometrica* 28 (January 1960): 1–29.

––––––. "A Permanent Income Theory for Investment: Some Empirical Explorations." *American Economic Review* 57 (June 1967): 363–390.

Eisner, R., and M. I. Nadiri. "On Investment Behavior and Neoclassical Theory." *Review of Economics and Statistics* 50 (August 1968): 369–382.

Eisner, R., and R. H. Strotz. "Determinants of Business Investment." In Commission on Money and Credit. *Impacts of Monetary Policy.* Englewood Cliffs, N.J., Prentice-Hall, 1963.

Fair, R. C. *The Short-Run Demand Function for Workers and Hours.* Amsterdam, North-Holland, 1969.

Feldstein, M. "Specification of the Labour Input in the Aggregate Production Function." *Review of Economic Studies* 34 (October 1967): 375–386.

Fisher, M. "Aggregate Production Functions and the Explanation of Wages: A Simulation Experiment." *Review of Economics and Statistics* 53 (November 1971): 305–325.

Friedman, M. *A Theory of the Consumption Function*. Princeton, N.J., Princeton University Press, 1957.

Gould, J. P. "Adjustment Costs in the Theory of Investment of the Firm." *Review of Economic Studies* 35 (January 1968): 47–55.

Griliches, Z. "Distributed Lags: A Survey." *Econometrica* 35 (January 1967): 16–49.

———. "Capital-Skill Complementarity." *Review of Economics and Statistics* 51 (November 1969): 465–468.

Griliches, Z., and N. Wallace. "The Determinants of Investment Revisited." *International Economic Review* 6 (September 1965): 311–329.

Hall, R., and D. Jorgenson. "Tax Policy and Investment Behavior." *American Economic Review* 57 (June 1967): 391–414.

Hickman, B. *Investment Demand and U.S. Economic Growth*. Washington, D.C., The Brookings Institution, 1965.

Holt, C., F. Modigliani, J. Muth, and H. Simon. *Planning Production, Inventories, and Work Force*. Englewood Cliffs, N.J., Prentice-Hall, 1960.

Hultgren, T. *Costs, Prices, and Profits: Their Cyclical Relations*. New York, NBER, 1965.

Ireland, J. J., and D. J. Smyth. "Short-Run Employment Functions in Australian Manufacturing." *Review of Economics and Statistics* 69 (November 1967): 537–544.

Johnston, J. *Econometric Methods*. New York, McGraw-Hill, 1963.

Jorgenson, D. "Capital Theory and Investment Behavior." *American Economic Review* 53 (May 1963): 247–259.

Jorgenson, D., and S. S. Handel. "Investment Behavior in U.S. Regulated Industries." *Bell Journal of Economics and Management Science* 2 (Spring 1971): 213–264.

Jorgenson, D., J. Hunter, and M. I. Nadiri. "A Comparison of Alternative Econometric Models of Quarterly Investment Behavior." *Econometrica* 38 (March 1970): 187–212.

———. "The Predictive Performance of Econometric Models of Quarterly Investment Behavior." *Econometrica* 38 (March 1970): 213–224.

Jorgenson, D., and C. D. Siebert. "Optimal Capital Accumulation and Corporate Investment Behavior." *Journal of Political Economy* 76 (November/December 1968): 1123–1151.

Jorgenson, D., and J. A. Stephenson. "The Time Structure of Investment Behavior in U.S. Manufacturing, 1947–60." *Review of Economics and Statistics* 49 (February 1967): 16–27.

Klein, L. R. "Studies in Investment Behavior." In *Conference on Business Cycles*. New York, NBER, 1951, pp. 233–303.

Klein, L. R., and R. S. Preston. "The Measurement of Capacity Utilization." *American Economic Review* 57 (March 1967): 34–58.

Koyck, L. M. *Distributed Lags and Investment Analysis*. Amsterdam, North-Holland, 1954.

Kuh, E. "Cyclical and Secular Labor Productivity in U.S. Manufacturing." *Review of Economics and Statistics* 47 (February 1965a): 1–12.

———. "Income Distribution and Employment Over the Business Cycle." In J. Duesenberry et al., eds. *The Brookings Quarterly Econometric Model of the United States*. Chicago, Rand-McNally, 1965b.

Lewis, H. *Unionism and Relative Wages in the United States: An Empirical Inquiry*. Chicago, University of Chicago Press, 1963.

Lovell, M. C. "Department Store Inventory, Sales, and Order Relationships." In J. Duesenberry et al., eds. *The Brookings Model: Some Further Results*. Amsterdam, North-Holland, 1969.

Lucas, R. E. "Optimal Investment Policy and the Flexible Accelerator." *International Economic Review* 8 (February 1967): 78–85.

Marris, R. *Economics of Capital Utilization*. Cambridge, Engl., Cambridge University Press, 1964.

Mayer, T. "Plant and Equipment Lead Times." *Journal of Business* 33 (April 1960): 127–132.

Mayor, T. H. "Equipment Expenditures by Input-Output Industries." *Review of Economic Statistics* 53 (February 1971): 26–36.

Meyer, J., and R. R. Glauber. *Investment Decisions, Economic Forecasting, and Public Policy*. Cambridge, Harvard University Press, 1964.

Meyer, J., and E. Kuh. *The Investment Decision: An Empirical Inquiry*. Cambridge, Harvard University Press, 1957.

Mills, E. A. *Price, Output, and Inventory Policy: A Study in the Economics of the Firm and Industry*. Publications in Operations Research 7. New York, Wiley, 1962.

Muth, J. F. "Optimal Properties of Exponentially Weighted Forecasts." *Journal of the American Statistical Association* 55 (June 1960): 299–306.

Nadiri, M. I. "Rate of Utilization, Relative Prices, and Investment Behavior." New York, NBER, 1969. Processed.

————. "The Effects of Relative Prices and Capacity on the Demand for Labor in the U.S. Manufacturing Sector." *Review of Economic Studies* 35 (July 1968): 273–288.

————. "Some Approaches to the Theory and Measurement of Total Factor Productivity: A Survey." *Journal of Economic Literature* 8 (December 1970): 1137–1177.

Nadiri, M. I., and S. Rosen. "Interrelated Factor Demand Functions." *American Economic Review* 59 (September 1969): 457–471.

Nerlove, M. "Notes on the Production and Derived Demand Relations Included in Macro-Econometric Models." *International Economic Review* 8 (June 1967): 223–242.

————. "Distributed Lags and Unobserved Components in Economic Time Series." In W. Fellner et al., eds. *Ten Economic Studies in the Tradition of Irving Fisher.* New York, Wiley, 1967(a).

————. "Recent Empirical Studies of the CES and Related Production Functions." In M. Brown, ed. *The Theory and Empirical Analysis of Production.* New York, NBER, 1967(b).

————. "On Lags in Economic Behavior." Abstracted in *Econometrica* (July 1971).

Oi, W. "Labor as a Quasi-Fixed Factor." *Journal of Political Economy* 70 (October 1962): 538–555.

Phelps, E., et al., eds. *Micro-economic Foundations of Employment and Inflation Theory.* New York, Norton, 1970.

Popkin, J. "The Relationship between New Orders and Shipments: An Analysis of the Machinery and Equipment Industries." *Survey of Current Business* 45 (March 1965): 24–32.

Rosen, S. "Short-Run Employment Variation on Class-I Railroads in the United States." *Econometrica* 36 (July 1968): 511–529.

————. "On the Interindustry Wage and Hours Structure." *Journal of Political Economy* 77 (March/April 1969): 249–273.

Schramm, R. "The Influence of Relative Prices, Production Conditions, and Adjustment Costs on Investment Behavior." *Review of Economic Studies* 37 (July 1970): 361–376.

Sims, C. "Are There Variables in Short-Run Production Relations?" *Annals of Economic and Social Measurement* 1 (January 1972): 17–36.

Soligo, R. "The Short-Run Relationship Between Employment and Output." *Yale Economic Essays* 6 (Spring 1966): 161–215.

Solow, R. "The Short-Run Productivity Puzzle." Cambridge, MIT Press, 1970. Processed.

Stigler, G., and J. Kindahl. *The Behavior of Industrial Prices*. New York, NBER, 1970.

Treadway, A. "Optimal Entrepreneurial Behavior and Distributed Lag in Investment Equations." Evanston, Ill., Northwestern University, November 1966. Processed.

————. "On Rational Entrepreneurial Behavior and the Demand for Investment." *Review of Economic Studies* 36 (April 1969): 227–240.

U.S. Department of Commerce. *Survey of Current Business*. Various issues.

————. *Manufacturers' Shipments, Inventories, and New Orders, 1961–68*. Series M3–1.1, 1968.

————. *National Income and Product Accounts of the United States, 1929–65*. 1966.

U.S. Department of Labor. *Earnings and Employment for the United States, 1909–65*. 1965.

Zabel, E. "A Dynamic Model of the Competitive Firm." *International Economic Review* 8 (June 1967): 194–208.

Zarnowitz, V. "Unfilled Orders, Price Changes, and Business Fluctuations." *Review of Economics and Statistics* 40 (November 1962): 367–394.

Index